"Solid scholarship, sensitive teaching, deep faith—these outstanding qualities of Robert Mounce's ministry are combined in WHAT ARE WE WAITING FOR?

"The message of Revelation with its call to courage, patience, and hope in the midst of devilry was never more needed than it is today. WHAT ARE WE WAITING FOR? will drive that message home to all who love the Scriptures as effectively as any book I know."

Dr. David Hubbard
Fuller Seminary

# THE BOOK OF
# REVELATION

## A LAYMAN'S COMMENTARY AND STUDY GUIDE

# What Are We Waiting For?

## DR. ROBERT MOUNCE

David C. Cook Publishing Co.

ELGIN, ILLINOIS—WESTON, ONTARIO

WHAT ARE WE WAITING FOR?
© 1979 David C. Cook Publishing Co.
All rights reserved. Except for brief excerpts for review purposes, no part of
this book may be reproduced without written permission from the publisher.

All Scripture quotations are from the New International Version.

Published by David C. Cook Publishing Co., Elgin, IL 60120
Cover design by Kurt Dietsch

Printed in the United States of America

ISBN 0-89191-129-4
LC 79-50068

# Contents

# Preface

WHAT ARE WE WAITING FOR? takes as its basic English text the *New International Version* of the New Testament. This translation has a number of advantages, particularly the fact that it is a recent and reliable piece of work done by evangelical scholars, working together within a committee structure. It may well become the standard biblical text for conservative Christianity.

This layman's commentary and study guide is designed to be of help to the person who wants to learn what the Book of Revelation is all about. It emphasizes the major themes of Revelation and how they relate to the way Christians are to live. It is not as technical and extensive as my commentary on Revelation in the *New International Commentary on the New Testament* series. The larger work was the fruit of some fifteen years of careful study of the Greek text, and discusses in detail a number of issues of less interest to the general reader.

The questions at the end of each chapter cause the reader to pay close attention to the text of Scripture itself. They also help the reader develop a unified approach to the book as a whole and arrive at a personal understanding and application of Revelation's central truths.

My deepest appreciation goes to an office staff that has given invaluable help in typing and proofreading the manuscript, specifically Mary Ann McGehee, Lynne Nave, and Nelda Steen.

# Introduction

I HAVE A THEORY about the Book of Revelation that runs counter to popular opinion. It is usually met with a "what's-that-again?" response. I believe that the Book of Revelation is no more difficult to understand than any other book of the New Testament when it is approached properly.

Unfortunately people have been conditioned to believe either that the book is totally incomprehensible or that it is decipherable only by a select few who have special insight into prophecy.

Now doesn't it seem a bit strange that God would veil the final chapter of human history so that only a few pundits could discover how it will all turn out? Revelation was originally written to be read aloud in the seven churches of Asia.

In the very first paragraph we find the promise "Blessed is the one who reads the words of this prophecy, and blessed are those who hear it and take to heart what is written in it" (1:3). But how can we "take to heart" what we don't understand? Obviously, something is awry.

Could the problem stem from our tendency to approach the book by asking the wrong questions? So often our primary concern is to identify images such as the four living creatures, the rider of the white horse, and the seventh head of the beast. Some of the images can and should be identified. However, even when all the figures are labeled and all the riddles solved, the essential message of the book may not have been uncovered. By focusing on details as if that were the major interpretive task, many have completely missed the central significance of this book

There is a simple way to prove that the fundamental truths of Revelation are not difficult. For the moment, put away all your curiosity about the details, get comfortable, and read it through at one sitting, which will take about an hour. Then take a piece of paper and write down the basic themes of the book from memory.

I'll miss my guess if you don't include most of the following: the need for believers to remain faithful in these perilous times, the vicious activity of Satan against the people of God, the sovereignty of God as he guides the world to its conclusion, the return of Christ to vindicate his followers, the punishment of the wicked, and the blessedness of the eternal state when all sin will have been removed. This is the message of Revelation. It is almost impossible to miss unless undue concern for detail has dulled our normal sense of what is significant.

This book is like a huge painting of the end times. Move up too close to examine each brush stroke, and the grandeur of the painting disappears. It must be viewed in its entirety. Because it communicates the great truths of the close of redemptive history. It requires perspective. An obsession with the quality of canvas or the exact shade of paint in a particular corner makes it impossible to grasp the artist's larger vision. Revelation is not for the prosaic, who would expend their energies arguing trivia. It is for those who wish to experience the wonder of God's sovereign control over the course of man's history.

# REVELATION ONE

IN SCHOOL WE LEARNED that a paragraph should contain no more than one basic idea. When an author changes the subject, a new paragraph should begin. This rule is helpful in interpreting Scripture.

The first chapter of Revelation contains ten paragraphs. The longest has six sentences (vv. 12-16), and the shortest only one word, *John* (v. 4a). The general approach of this commentary will be to summarize each major unit (often more than one paragraph) in a single sentence, and then comment on certain details to help clarify the basic theological or ethical truths.

**1-3**

Through his servant John, God has revealed what must soon take place and pronounces a blessing on all who hear and take to heart what the prophet has written.

Many people assume that the Second Coming of Christ dominates the Book of Revelation. They are surprised to discover that the Parousia, or Second Coming, doesn't come until chapter 19, where it is dealt with in a few short verses that portray the event somewhat differently from the familiar passage in 1 Thessalonians (4:14-17).

The book is not so much an unveiling (that is what the word *revelation* means) *of* Jesus Christ as it is a revelation made possible *by* him. In chapter 5 we will learn that only the Lamb is worthy to break the seals on the scroll of destiny and disclose how it will all turn out.

Note that John—an important link in the chain of revelation—testifies to everything he "saw." The many visions, beginning at chapter 4 and continuing to the end of the book, were actually *seen* by John. They are not his attempts to put some of his ideas into a current literary genre, which we now call apocalyptic.

Like his master, Jesus Christ, he is a "faithful witness" (v. 5). No wonder the local reader and those who listen (and take it to heart) are blessed. The time is near. Persecution is just around the corner. In fact, Antipas of Pergamum has already been martyred (2:13). It is blessed to know that in spite of all earthly and Satanic opposition, God remains sovereign. At the appointed time, he will put an end to evil and reward those who have faithfully persevered.

**4-5a**

In ancient days letters began with the name of the writer. This letter is from John (the apostle, I believe) and is sent to seven specific churches in the Roman province of Asia, the western half of modern Turkey. In chapters 2 and 3, we will find a series of seven brief letters, each addressed to a separate church. But all seven will accompany the main body of the book as it is circulated to each church. The seven churches form a rough geographic circle and were perhaps major postal centers in Asia.

Grace and peace are pronounced upon the churches from a threefold source. God the Father is portrayed as existing in all time (past, present, and future), and Jesus Christ is shown as the faithful witness, resurrected from the dead, and sovereign over the kings of the earth. Each title is intended to support and encourage the believer in the coming trial, when the state will demand that everyone worship the emperor. Some writers think that "the seven spirits before his throne" represent the Holy Spirit (Isa. 11:2 is usually quoted); but it is simpler to take them as heavenly beings (see the three other places they are mentioned—3:1; 4:5; 5:6).

### 5b-8

It is characteristic of the prologue and the epilogue (1:1-9 and 22:6-21) to place a series of separate yet related utterances side by side. In verses 5b-8 we find a doxology, an exclamation of Christ's Second Coming and a declaration by God of his eternal existence.

The doxologies of Revelation (and there are a number of them: 4:11; 5:9; 12f; 7:10; etc.) are spontaneous outbursts of praise and gratitude. This first one is directed toward Christ, who loves us (present tense) and has freed us from our sins (accomplished in the past). Christ has set us free by his death. The children of Israel were set free from bondage in Egypt and promised on Mount Sinai that if they would keep the commandments of God, they would be "a kingdom of priests and a holy nation" (Exod. 19:5-6). In a "second exodus," Christ frees believers to be the new people of God.

The return of Christ will be seen by all. There is no secret rapture here! As Jesus said, "All the nations of the earth . . . will see the Son of Man coming on the clouds of the sky" (Matt. 24:30). The people of the earth (unbelievers) will mourn, not out of repentance, but because his return discloses the judgment of God (16:9, 11, 21).

Alpha and omega are the first and last letters of the Greek alphabet. It is simply another way of emphasizing God's sovereign control over all that happens, from the beginning of time until the end. He is almighty, an important fact to remember in times of crisis.

**9-11**

John had been exiled to the island of Patmos, a small, rugged island in the Aegean Sea, about fifty miles southwest of Ephesus. Apparently John's preaching was making it difficult for the local authorities to propagate emperor worship, so they had banished him. On the Lord's day, he receives a divine commission to write down what he is about to see and send it to the seven churches of Asia.

John identifies himself closely with his Christian brothers on the mainland. He shares with them the suffering involved in fidelity to Christ and the hope of a future kingdom of blessedness.

The Lord's day was the first day of the week. It is *his* day because on it he rose victorious over death. To be "in the Spirit" means to be caught up in meditation about the things of the Spirit. While in this state of spiritual exaltation, John hears a loud voice, clear as a trumpet, instructing him to write what he sees and to send it to the churches on the mainland. The seven churches are both historic congregations and symbols of the strengths and weaknesses of churches throughout time. I do not think they prophesy seven successive periods of church history.

**12-16**

What a surprise when John turns to see who has spo-

13

ken to him! There in the midst of seven golden lampstands stands one "like a son of man," priestly in dress and overpowering in appearance. He holds seven stars in his right hand and a double-edged sword in his mouth.

Most writers go into great detail to show what each descriptive phrase symbolizes. Our approach will be to resist this temptation. It is more important to reflect on the total impact of the vision than to research the possible background of each item, although this is appropriate for scholarly commentaries. The total vision is this: long robe with golden sash, burnished feet, pure white hair, penetrating eyes, and a deep vibrant voice. What an impact this awe-inspiring figure must have had on the aged disciple!

**17-20**

John falls to the ground. He is immediately reassured by the sovereign Lord and commissioned to record the visions he will receive. During the earthly life of Jesus, John had a somewhat similar experience. When he was on a mountaintop with Jesus, he watched our Lord's transfiguration. A voice from heaven spoke, and "when the disciples heard this, they fell face down to the ground, terrified." Jesus touched them and told them not to fear (Matt. 17:1-8).

In verse 8 God called himself "the Alpha and the Omega." Jesus makes the same claim with the parallel expression "the First and the Last." Both titles emphasize sovereignty. Everything is under control. Having conquered death through the resurrection, Jesus is now "the Living One." As the keeper of the keys of death and Hades, he has complete control over their power to terrorize and enslave.

Verse 19 is often taken as setting forth a threefold outline for the book. "What you have seen" would be the vision just experienced. "What is now" refers to the seven letters in chapters 2 and 3. "What will take place later" is everything from chapter 4 on. Unfortunately, the book doesn't fall into such a neat pattern.

It is preferable to take the initial clause as a repetition of the earlier command ("Write on a scroll what you see," v. 11) and the two other clauses as indicating what is to be written.

Our first clue for interpretation comes from Christ himself. The "seven lampstands" are the seven congregations to which the book is being sent. The "seven stars" are seven angels or messengers of the churches, a reference to the local elder of each church or possibly to the prevailing spirit of each congregation.

## QUESTIONS

1. Who is the revealer in the Book of Revelation?
2. What is the immediate purpose of this revelation?
3. Why should we visualize a congregational situation in verse 3?
4. Who is the one "who is, and who was, and who is to come?"
5. In what sense is Jesus the "firstborn from the dead"?
6. How has Jesus freed us?
7. What is the purpose of our being "a kingdom and priests"?
8. Who will see Jesus when he returns?
9. Do you think "those who pierced him" refers only to the Roman soldiers who nailed Jesus to the cross? If not, how have others (including ourselves) "pierced him"?
10. Why was it important for believers in Asia Minor at

that particular time to be assured that God was "the Almighty"?

11. What are the indications that John, the "arch-bishop" of Asia Minor, did not place himself above those to whom he ministered?

12. What shows that John had faithfully proclaimed his message in spite of threatened dangers?

13. Who was the one "like a son of man" who stood surrounded by the seven golden lampstands?

14. If you had an encounter with the glorified Christ, would your response have been any different from John's? If so, in what way?

15. In what way do verses 8 and 17 indicate the equality of God the Father and God the Son?

16. Why can death no longer imprison the Christian believer?

17. Explain the mystery of the seven stars and the seven lampstands. How can this interpretive clue aid in understanding the rest of the book?

18. What major insight from chapter 1 will help you in your Christian walk this coming week?

# REVELATION
# TWO

THE NEXT TWO CHAPTERS consist of separate letters to seven different churches in Asia. Since all seven go to each congregation, they may be considered as letters within a letter. When compared side by side, a striking similarity in form emerges. They all contain:

    charge to write,

    identification of author,

    acknowledgment of positive achievements,

    words of encouragement, censure, counsel, or
      warning,

    exhortation to hear, and a

    promise to the overcomer.

Each letter, however, is tailored to the immediate

needs of the historical church being addressed. I do not think the letters predict the course of church history, but they do reveal the strengths and weaknesses of the church universal.

**1**

Note that in each letter the author (the glorified and triumphant Christ) is identified by a particular phrase or clause taken from the opening vision in chapter 1. In each case, the choice is appropriate. To Ephesus he is the one who walks among the seven golden lampstands and holds the seven stars in his right hand. Taking a clue from Revelation 1:20, this would mean that Christ is present in the midst of the congregation and holds them in his control.

**2-3**

Ephesus was a hard-working church that had maintained doctrinal purity. In a day when churches were frequently infiltrated by self-styled apostles, intent on manipulating local congregations for personal advantage, Ephesus had put them to the test and rejected all pretenders. Commitment to Christ had worked economic and social hardships on believers, yet they persevered and had not grown weary.

**4-6**

Someone has said that our greatest weakness inevitably lies in the area of our major strength. This was true of Ephesus. The critical faculties, which made the church sensitive to any indication of doctrinal deviation, had created a climate of suspicion in which brotherly love was noticeably absent. The major fault of the congregation was that they had forsaken their first love. That first outflowing affection for God and the rich relationship of mutual concern among their membership was lost. Christ admonishes them to remember the warm affection of former days, repent of their coldness, and do those things that flow naturally from a context of love and concern. If not, Christ will come in judgment.

Then, lest the censure seem too severe, he commends them for hating the practices of the Nicolaitans, a heretical group who wanted the church to work out a compromise with paganism by eating food that had been sacrificed to idols and taking part in sexual immorality (for evidence of the same sect in Pergamum and Thyatira, see 2:14-15, 20.)

**7**

Each letter contains the exhortation, "He who has an ear, let him hear what the Spirit says to the churches." It is crucial that believers actually *hear* (that is, hear and take to heart) what the Spirit says. Note that while Christ dictates the letter, it is the Spirit who speaks to the inner man. To overcome is to obey what the Spirit says. And to the overcomer, Christ gives the right to eat of the tree of life (a symbol of immortality, see Gen. 3:22-24). This is a promise to restore the fellowship with God enjoyed by Adam and Eve before the Fall.

**8-11**

The letter to Smyrna is the shortest of the seven. Unlike the others (except Philadelphia) it contains no note of censure. This is significant in view of the fact that the city of Smyrna was exceptionally pro-Roman, and Christians living there had experienced intense hostility. The most famous early church father to be martyred was the elderly Polycarp, the "twelfth martyr in Smyrna."

Christ identifies himself to the believers at Smyrna as "the First and the Last, who died and came to life again." This assurance of divine sovereignty and victory over death would strengthen the church for the difficult period ahead. Christ is fully aware of their "afflictions and ... poverty." Apparently their faithfulness to the gospel had already brought economic hardship. Yet spiritually they were rich.

Christ also knew the slanderous accusations of those who claimed to be Jews. We recall Paul's teaching that a real Jew was not one who had simply undergone the outward act of circumcision but one who had experienced the inward cleansing of the Spirit (Rom. 2: 28-29). These slanderers belonged to the synagogue of Satan, not the synagogue of God—a powerful denunciation of the local Jewish settlement!

The believers at Smyrna were about to enter a new and more intense period of suffering. They were to be cast into prison by the devil (the "chief rabbi" of the synagogue of Satan?). There they would suffer persecution for ten days.

Numbers in Revelation are normally symbolic. We have already encountered seven churches, seven lampstands, and seven angels. The number seven will be repeated many times in Revelation and rather regularly symbolizes completeness. Other numbers occurring frequently are four, ten, and one thousand. Ten days may represent a short period and perhaps be related in some indirect way to the 1,000-year millennium of chapter 20. The admonition for this time of trial (suffering is a form of testing) is to remain faithful, even unto death. As a result those who endure will receive the "crown of life"—that is, the victor's wreath, which is life.

Following the exhortation to hear, the overcomer is promised immunity against the second death. In chapter 20 the second death is equated with the lake of fire (v. 14b). To remain faithful during persecution is to overcome, and Christ promises eternal life to overcomers.

**12-13**

Because Pergamum was the provincial capital of Asia,

it had been granted by Rome the "right of the sword," the authority to execute at will. To this particular congregation, then, Christ is the one who has "the sharp, double-edged sword" (see 1:16). The ultimate power of life and death belongs not to Roman magistrates but to God.

Reference to the throne of Satan reflects the fact that Pergamum had become the official Asian center for emperor worship. Satan ruled from Rome in the West and Pergamum in the East. Yet believers in this citadel of paganism had remained faithful to Christ, even though one of their number, Antipas, had been martyred for his faithful witness. (Legend has it that he was roasted to death in a brazen bull.)

**14-16**

Pergamum, however, was not without fault. Some of its members held to the teaching of Balaam. From Numbers (25:1ff and 31:16), we learn that Balaam had led Israel into apostasy through the seductive activity of Midianite women.

Like the ancient Israelites, some at Pergamum had been enticed into taking part in pagan feasts and the accompanying immorality. Balaam stands as a symbol of all false teachers who urge compromise with the lax standards of the worldly community. The Nicolaitans (v. 15) are probably another reference to the same group.

Christ admonishes the church at Pergamum to repent of its indifference to this heretical development. Pergamum's weakness is opposite of that at Ephesus, where doctrine was jealously guarded at the expense of love. Failure to take action will result in a divine visitation of judgment against the offenders.

**17**

To the overcomer Christ promises hidden manna and a white stone inscribed with a new name. Manna was the food supplied by God to the Israelites during their long journey from Egypt to the promised land. Hidden manna seems to refer to the heavenly, messianic banquet that awaits all God's people at the end of this age.

The white stone could be an allusion to the ancient custom of using *tessera*, little tablets of wood, stone, or metal, for a variety of purposes. Here it would serve as a token for admission to the heavenly banquet. The new name, known only to him who receives it, is the name of each faithful believer.

## 18-19

To the Thyatiran church Christ presents himself as "the Son of God" with eyes like blazing fire and feet like burnished brass. Some writers see an intentional contrast with Apollo, the guardian diety of Thyatira. Christ, not Apollo, is the true Son of God. His piercing gaze can see through the cunning arguments of Jezebel as he stands strong and able to carry out his judgment.

Before giving a lengthy reprimand for error, Christ acknowledges the church's love and faith, service and perseverance. The latter works grow out of, and are an expression of, the former. Unlike the Ephesian church, who forsook its first love and was admonished to "do the things you did at first" (2:5), the Thyatirans were "now doing more than they did at first."

## 20-25

Like Pergamum, there were those at Thyatira who held to the teaching of Balaam. A woman was influencing believers to compromise their commitment to God, like her Old Testament counterpart, Jezebel. This wicked queen of Ahab had encouraged the Israelites into idolatrous worship of the Canaanite Baal (1 Kings 16:29ff; 2 Kings 9:30ff).

The Thyatiran "Jezebel" had persuaded a portion of the local congregation to compromise with the local cult by taking part in their religious feasts and sexual immorality. She may have reasoned that in a city noted for its many trade guilds (which were inseparably interwoven with cultic ceremonies), it would be economic suicide to reject the minimum requirements for membership. Since "we know that an idol is nothing at all" (1 Cor. 8:4), what harm could come from agreeing to their simple requests? The fact that she claimed the gift of prophecy and had convinced others of this suggests that she was a woman of prominence and possessed considerable persuasive power.

This New Testament Jezebel has been given time to repent of her adulterous relationship with the pagan culture, but has refused to do so. Consequently, she is to be cast into a bed of suffering, and her paramours are to suffer intensely unless they repent. From 1 Corinthians 11:27-30, we learn that sickness and even death were supposed to result from spiritual offenses. Jezebel's "children" were all who embraced her doctrine. The judgment of God will fall upon them all, and then the churches throughout Asia will understand that Christ really does search the heart and mind, repaying every man according to his works. The doctrine of judgment based on works is taught in both the Old and New Testaments (see Jer. 17:10; Matt. 16:27; Rom. 2:6).

Those at Thyatira who have not been taken in by Jezebel are admonished to hold on to what they have until Christ comes. No other burden will be placed upon them. These are they who "have not learned Satan's so-called deep secrets." This phrase is sometimes taken as a satirical response to the sect's claim of knowing the deep things of God. Or it may be a reference to the Gnostic boast that only by entering into Satan's realm (in this case, by eating at his sacred feast and indulging one's sexual appetites) can the Christian emerge victorious and demonstrate complete freedom from Satan's power.

**26-29**

The overcomer, he who does Christ's will to the end, is promised authority over the nations. This promise of ruling the nations is a way of saying that in the new age about to break, the tables will be turned: this Christian minority will no longer be under pressure from Roman authorities. The righteous will rule over the wicked.

Ruling with a rod of iron (the Greek word is "to shepherd") in this context refers to the shepherd's wielding of an iron-tipped club or staff against preying beasts. The power of secular authority is to be shattered like a broken vessel of clay. The overcomer will also receive the "morning star"—perhaps an allusion to the era of eternal righteousness, which is about to dawn.

## QUESTIONS

1. What does it mean that Christ "walks among the seven lampstands" and "holds the seven stars in his right hand"?
2. Was it appropriate for the church at Ephesus to test men who claimed to be apostles? Why or why not?
3. What was the basic fault of the Ephesian church?
4. Do you think that attention to correct doctrine necessarily works against maintaining a warm, personal relationship with God?
5. How can memory help to regain a previous level of spiritual life?
6. What would happen to the Ephesian congregation if it failed to repent? What does that mean?
7. In what way, if any, does your present love for God differ from your initial relationship with him?

8. What group will have the right to "eat from the tree of life"?

9. In what way were the Christians at Smyrna rich?

10. What does it take to be a "real Jew"?

11. What should be the Christian attitude toward suffering for Christ?

12. What is required for receiving the crown of life?

13. If Satan's throne is his place of power and influence, what aspects of contemporary culture are affected by his rule?

14. What do you imagine would take place if all Christians in America were called upon to renounce their faith or suffer the consequences? Do you think this could happen within our lifetime?

15. What is "the teaching of Balaam"?

16. What would be a contemporary equivalent to the doctrine of the Nicolaitans?

17. How does Christ deal with the church that tolerates doctrinal error and immoral conduct?

18. To what do the "hidden manna" and "white stone" refer?

19. Why did John call the heretical prophetess of Thyatira Jezebel?

20. How could the followers of Jezebel escape divine judgment?

21. What is promised to the overcomer at Thyatira? If this is to be interpreted literally, when would it probably take place?

22. Which of the strengths (or weaknesses) mentioned in the first four letters are most characteristic of your local congregation?

23. Which of the first four churches would you rather join? Why?

# REVELATION
# THREE

TO THE CHURCH AT SARDIS Christ presents himself as
the one "who holds the seven spirits of God and the
seven stars." In chapter 2, verse 1, we learned that holding the seven stars indicates Christ's sovereign control
over the churches. That he now holds the seven spirits
of God means that this sovereign control extends to
heavenly beings, which are in some way related to the
churches (see 1:4).

**1-3**

Christ knows the deeds of the congregation at Sardis,
and there is nothing to commend. They have the reputation of being alive but are dead. It would appear that
they have so completely come to terms with their pagan

environment that there is no longer anything about them to offend anyone. They exist rather comfortably as a Christian church (in name, at least) but are, in fact, spiritually dead. Wake up while there is still hope, exhorts Christ.

The history of Sardis provides an interesting parallel to their spiritual lethargy. The acropolis there was situated on a spur on Mount Tmolus and accessible only from the south side. On the other three sides, the sheer rock cliffs dropped some fifteen hundred feet to the valley below. It was a natural citadel, essentially inaccessible. Yet twice in its history, enemy groups had scaled the walls and captured the city. A false sense of security led to lack of vigilance. In a spiritual sense as well, they had grown lax. Unless they awake immediately and shore up their defenses, they will fall to the enemy.

Once again memory is summoned as an aid to renewal. The church is to hear, obey, and repent. If not, Christ will appear as suddenly as a thief. Like the daring Cretan who scaled the cliffs with fifteen men to open the gates and allow the armies of Antiochus to capture the fort, Christ will appear suddenly in judgment.

**4-6**

Yet even in the complacent church of Sardis, there were some who had not soiled their clothes. They are to walk with Christ in white. In context, soiling one's clothes would refer to defiling involvement with the local, pagan religious practices. White clothes speak of justification. The few who have not soiled their faith by compromise will walk with Christ in the pure garments of righteousness.

To overcome is to remain true, and that keeps one's name in the book of life. In Exodus 32: 32-33, Moses pled with God for the wayward Israelites, saying that he wished to be blotted out "of the book you have written" if the people's sins were not forgiven. The idea of a divine register was common in Jewish thought.

What it means in the New Testament to be blotted out of this book of life is not clear. The various answers proposed by those who bring the verse into conformity with a doctrine of "eternal security" are not especially persuasive. It is better to let the warning stand as it is, recognizing that doctrines are not to be built from phrases taken from figurative writing.

A third promise to the overcomer is that Christ will acknowledge his name before God and the angels. During his earthly ministry, Jesus had promised his followers that if they acknowledged him before men, he would acknowledge them before the Father (Matt. 10:32).

**7-10**

Philadelphia was the city of brotherly love. It took its name from Attalus II Philadelphus, a Pergamene king who earned the title "lover of his brother" because of his legendary devotion to his older brother Eumenes II. Philadelphia and Smyrna are the only two churches that receive unqualified praise from Christ.

To the Philadelphians, Christ writes as the true Messiah, who exercises absolute control over entrance to the eternal Kingdom. In both the Old and New Testaments, God is called the Holy One (see Isa. 40:25; John 6:69). The "key of David" stands for complete control over the royal household. Whatever the person who holds the key opens or shuts cannot be changed.

Christ has placed before the church an "open door." This is often taken as indicating the opportunity for missionary activity. Another interpretation fits the context better. The congregation is a small one ("you have little strength") and has remained faithful in spite of Jewish opposition. These adversaries are labeled "liars" and their place of worship is called the "synagogue of Satan." They would undoubtedly have excommunicated any of their group who confessed Jesus as Messiah. Never mind, says Christ, although the synagogue door has been shut in your face, the door to the eternal Kingdom of God has been opened wide for you. No one can shut that door!

The time will come when those who have put you out will come to you, acknowledging that you are the ones loved by the Messiah. Verse 9 does not envision a cringing response of defeated enemies. It is an Oriental metaphor depicting the response of antagonists to the vindication of the church and its faith.

A time of great testing will come to "those who live on the earth." The reference here and elsewhere in Revelation (6:10; 8:13; 11:10; 13:8; 17:8) is to the enemies of the church. This "hour of trial" is the three-and a-half-year rule of Antichrist (13:5-10), which precedes the triumphal return of Christ to establish his eternal Kingdom.

Since the church had endured patiently the hardships of life in Philadelphia, Christ promises to keep them from the final testing that is to fall upon the enemies of God. Some take this as a promise that Christ will come in a preliminary way to remove the church prior to any suffering (this "rapture" is not specifically mentioned in Revelation). It is better to understand the phrase as a promise that in the final period of demonic assault upon the earth, believers will receive spiritual protection against the forces of evil. This is consistent with Jesus' words in John 17:15, "My prayer is not that you take them out of the world but that you protect them from the evil one."

**11-13**

The time of Christ's coming is not far off (see 1:1;

22:7, 12, 20). Hold what you have so no one will take your victor's wreath. As an overcomer you will be placed like a pillar, securely and permanently in the temple of God. To the city of Philadelphia, which was devastated by the famous earthquake of A.D. 17, the idea of permanence would be especially appealing.

The overcomer will also be inscribed with three names: the name of God indicates divine ownership; the name of God's city, the new Jerusalem, speaks of citizenship in the heavenly commonwealth; and Christ's new name suggests the full revelation of his character at the Second Coming. While present problems test the patience of believers, the future is bright and the rewards of faithfulness beyond compare.

**14-18**

We now come to the last of the seven churches, the church of Laodicea. The passage is well known because of its reference to lukewarmness and its invitation to open the door of the heart and allow Christ to enter (v. 20).

To the Laodiceans Christ writes as "the Amen." The title is an affirmation of the trustworthiness of Christ, perhaps in contrast to the lack of faithfulness on their part. Since Jesus was faithful and true to his witness he now rules God's creation.

The basic fault of the Laodicean church is that it was lukewarm. This has been understood to mean that the church was neither spiritually hot nor cold, but had settled for an insipid lukewarmness.

It is regularly noted that several miles to the north, the hot mineral water from springs in Hieropolis spilled over the cliff above the Lycus and had covered the wide escarpment with a layer of white mineral. By the time the water reached the spillway, it had become lukewarm and was nauseous to the taste. The problem with this interpretation is that it is difficult to discern why it would be better to be spiritually cold than lukewarm.

The contrast appears to be between the medicinal waters of Hieropolis, which would provide healing, and the cool drinking water of Colossae, ten miles on up the Lycus glen, which would provide refreshment. The Laodiceans were "lukewarm" in the sense that their Christianity provided neither healing for the spiritually sick nor refreshment for those who were spiritually weary. They were offensive to God. He was about to vomit (the Greek verb is stronger than the New International Version, *spit* them out of his mouth. In their self-sufficiency, they viewed themselves as wealthy while, in fact, they were "wretched, pitiful, poor, blind, and naked." They were without any understanding of their true condition.

It has often been noted that Laodicea prided itself on its financial wealth (it rebuilt after a major earthquake without help from Rome), an extensive textile industry (its soft, black wool was internationally famous), and a popular eye salve (developed in connection with a renowned medical school). This is probably the background for Christ's admonition that they buy gold from him to become rich, white clothes to cover their nakedness, and salve to restore their sight. The areas of life that give them smug satisfaction are the very areas in which they need the greatest help!

**19-20**

One of the fundamental principles of divine training is that love may be expressed in rebuke and discipline (the Greek word means "to train as a child"). The proper response is to be earnest and repent. When God corrects, he takes his stand at the door of our heart and knocks. We must take the next step and open to him. When we respond, and only then, he enters and fellowship is restored or deepened. At no time does God force himself upon the believer.

This verse is often used in evangelism to portray God's desire to enter the heart of the unbeliever and bring salvation. It may be applied in this way. However, its primary reference is to believers whose lukewarmness provides neither healing to the sick nor refreshment to the weary. It is Christ's message to the self-sufficient who are unable to recognize their own poverty, shame, and blindness.

**21-22**

The promise that the overcomer will sit with Christ upon his throne is entirely eschatological. It belongs to the coming age. Jesus had promised his followers that in the age to come they would sit on twelve thrones, judging the tribes of Israel (Matt. 19:28).

In Revelation 6:10, the martyrs under the altar ask how long until their deaths are avenged. And in Chapter 20:4-6, they are raised to rule with Christ one-thousand years. While the figures are not to be pressed unduly, the scene predicted is one of universal recognition of the validity of God's people's faith and the benefits to follow.

## QUESTIONS

1. How can a church have the reputation of being alive and yet be dead?
2. In the context of verse 3, what is implied by Christ's assertion that he will "come like a thief"?
3. To what do "white garments" refer in the context of verse 4?
4. What is the "book of life"?
5. What is the "key of David"?
6. What is the "open door"?

7. Which phrases in verses 7 and 8 emphasize God's sovereignty?

8. On what basis did Christ refer to the Jewish synagogue in Philadelphia as "the synagogue of Satan"?

9. What will all unbelievers finally acknowledge about the Christian church?

10. What is the "hour of trial" about to come upon the earth?

11. Will believers be kept *physically* safe from the intense testing of the final days? If not, in what way are they to be kept "from the hour of trial"?

12. What does it mean to be inscribed with the name of God? What are the three names that will be inscribed on overcomers?

13. What does Christ mean when he calls the Laodicean Christians lukewarm?

14. What is God's response to lukewarmness? Do you think this is still his response?

15. Describe the Laodiceans' attitude toward their own spiritual attainments.

16. Why are love and discipline not contradictory?

17. What is the primary interpretive frame of reference for verse 20?

18. Why, in view of verse 20, can it be said that God is always a gentleman?

19. When will believers sit with Christ on his throne? What is the major point in this figure?

# REVELATION
# FOUR

THE SEVEN LETTERS to the churches of Asia are now
complete. All seven letters are to be sent to each congregation along with an account of the visions to follow.
1

John looks up from his scroll, and there before him
stands a door opening into heaven. The voice like a
trumpet, which had interrupted his meditation in the
previous chapter, now invites him up to heaven to learn
how God intends to bring history to a close and usher in
the eternal state. In the chapters that follow, we will
learn not only the events to take place but also the
activity of God (and Satan) that lies behind these events.

Some writers hold that the heavenly summons is to be

interpreted symbolically as the rapture of the church. There is nothing in the verse that supports this interpretation. Its purpose is to show John what must soon take place so he can report it to the churches (see 1:11; 1:1-2)—hardly a necessary action if the churches no longer exist on earth.

**2-4**

Immediately John is "in the Spirit" and beholds a throne room in heaven. The phrase describes a trancelike state appropriate for the visionary experiences to come. Prophetic ecstasy was not uncommon in Jewish literature (see 1 Kings 22:19; Acts 10:9-16). It is significant that the first thing John sees in heaven is a throne. This symbol, found more than forty times in Revelation, symbolizes power and authority. To churches about to enter a time of persecution, it was important to emphasize that God continues to be absolutely sovereign over the affairs of man. God, not Satan, is writing the final chapter of history.

God himself is not described. All we know is that on the throne sits one whose brilliance is like the light reflected from precious stones (Paul wrote that God "lives in unapproachable light" and is unseen by man, 1 Tim. 6:16).

Around the throne are twenty-four other thrones, upon which are seated twenty-four elders. Their identity has been widely debated. The rather popular view that they represent the entire people of God (the twelve patriarchs of the Old Testament and the twelve apostles of the New) is based upon inferior Greek manuscripts that alter the song the elders sing in chapter 5:9-10 to read "purchased us . . . made us to be . . . we will reign." In each case the proper pronouns are third person, not first ("purchased men . . . made them . . . they will reign").

35

# WHAT ARE WE WAITING FOR?

Since the elders speak of the people of God as a different and separate group in these verses, they should not be confused with that group. Most likely the elders are an order of exalted angelic beings who worship and serve God in the heavenly throne room.

**5-6a**

Before the throne are seven blazing lamps, which John identifies as the seven spirits of God (see 1:4). These also are angelic beings. In front of the throne stretches what appears to be a sea of crystal-clear glass. Rather than attaching a symbolic meaning to each item of the vision, it is better to understand many of the descriptive details as supporting the overall impression. A sea of glass reflecting the flashing brilliance of the emerald-colored rainbow around the throne would heighten the sense of God's transcendence and majesty. Lightning and thunder recall the appearance of God on Mount Sinai (Exod. 19:16) and occur regularly in similar scenes in Revelation (8:5; 11:19; 16:18).

**6b-8**

Between the throne and the circle of elders are four living creatures. Once again we are probably dealing with an angelic order. They are covered with eyes, which speaks of unceasing vigilance. Nothing escapes their notice. The first creature resembles a lion, the second an ox, the third has a face like a man, and the fourth is like an eagle in flight.

Reference is often made to the four cherubims of Ezekiel (1:5-6, 10), each of which had four faces (lion on the right, ox on the left, human in front, and eagle behind). The similarities and dissimilarities of the two passages illustrate how figures and symbols from the Old Testament are altered in some way when they enter into John's vision. Just as a dream often employs people and places known to the dreamer (usually with rather dramatic relocations and relationships), so John's visions build upon his familiarity with Jewish literature (the Old Testament and noncanonical materials).

It has been suggested that the four living creatures represent the entire animate creation. The fact that they take the form of various animals supports this conjecture. Yet their role as leaders in worship (4: 9-10; 5: 15) seems to assign to them a higher level of significance.

The description continues, noting that each of the four creatures had six wings and was covered with eyes (even under the wings). Since the eyes are mentioned twice (vv. 6 and 8), we may assume that what they symbolize is especially noteworthy. The many eyes indicate that the living creatures are totally alert to all that takes place in the throne room. They are the guardians of the throne of God. Any attempt to visualize the four creatures by taking the description in a strictly literal sense ends with bizarre configurations. This should remind us to concentrate on what the descriptions symbolize rather than the symbols themselves.

The living creatures are angelic beings who surround the throne and take part in unceasing worship of God. Night and day they proclaim the holiness of God, the one whose might exceeds all others and who not only is, but was, and is to come. To be caught up in adoration of God—the sovereign over all creation, seated upon the throne of the universe—is to understand who the living creatures are. The truth is dynamic and existential, not static and intellectual.

**9-11**

Whenever the living creatures praise and adore the one seated on the heavenly throne, the twenty-four elders prostrate themselves before the throne and worship God, who lives for ever and ever. These acts of spontaneous worship in no way contradict the ceaseless praise of verse 8. Revelation is written in a literary style that enjoys considerable freedom and ignores the rigid expectations of unimaginative prose.

In verse 8, the living creatures praised God for who he is. The twenty-four elders now declare him worthy of honor on the basis of what he did. He is worthy because he created all things. Elsewhere in John's writings, there are allusions to a heretical group, Gnostics, who held that God as spirit could have nothing to do with matter, which was intrinsically evil (see 1 John 4:1-3). The song of the elders corrects the dualistic idea that spirit and matter are essential opposites. God, who is spirit (John 4:24), created everything that is. It was his will to bring them into existence.

## QUESTIONS

1. Why was John summoned to the door of heaven?
2. Who is the one with a voice like a trumpet?
3. What does it mean to be "in the Spirit"?
4. What was the first thing John saw in heaven? What does it symbolize?
5. Who are the twenty-four elders?
6. With what are lightning and thunder in Scripture often connected? What is the Old Testament basis for this?
7. What (or who) are the "seven lamps"?
8. Describe the four living creatures.
9. Former writers used to equate the four living creatures with the four Gospels. What is your response to that interpretation?
10. How does the praise of the living creatures differ from that of the elders?

11. What was the Gnostic error of John's day, and how is it refuted by the song of the elders?

12. Chapter 4 is written against the background of worship in an ancient Eastern (or Oriental) culture. What would be the closest equivalent for worshiping and showing honor in a modern Western setting?

# REVELATION
# FIVE

JOHN'S ATTENTION is now drawn to a scroll in the right hand of God. Scrolls in ancient days were made by joining uniform sections of papyrus (the fibrous inner bark of a plant found in marshy areas along the Mediterranean) and rolling them onto a spindle. Normally they had writing only on the inside, where the fibers ran horizontally. The fact that this scroll had writing both in front and on the back indicates the fullness of its message.

1

The scroll was sealed with seven seals to guarantee that absolutely no one would be able to open it and discover what it contained. Years before, the prophet

Daniel was told to "close up and seal the words of the scroll until the time of the end" (Dan. 12:4). Now, however, the end is approaching, and the scroll of destiny must be opened.

**2-4**

But now a problem arises. Who is worthy to open the scroll and disclose the end of history? An angel proclaims the challenge in a loud voice so all can hear. But no one "in heaven or on earth or under the earth" is able to break the seals. The threefold division is not intended to teach a three-tiered universe. It is a way of stressing that everyone everywhere heard the proclamation (see Phil. 2:10 for a similar rhetorical division).

When no one is found worthy to open the scroll, John breaks out weeping. John does not weep because he is personally disappointed that he will not learn about the end, but because, unless the seals are broken, the end will be indefinitely postponed.

**5**

At that point, one of the elders speaks to John and tells him not to weep. There is one who has triumphed and is able to loose the seals and open the scroll. That person is "the Lion of the tribe of Judah, the Root of David." Both titles are taken from the Old Testament and had been interpreted messianically as referring to the coming Messiah. In Genesis 49, Jacob, in his final blessing upon his twelve sons, calls Judah "a lion's cub" and promises him authority "until he comes to whom it belongs" (vv. 9-10).

Centuries later Isaiah promises a "shoot . . . from the stump of Jesse," an ideal king from the line of David, who will bring to pass an era of peace (Isa. 11:1). Thus it is the Messiah himself who alone is worthy to break the seals and set into motion the consummation of history. He is worthy because he has triumphed. His triumph, as we shall learn in verses 9 and 10, is victory through the sacrifice of himself.

**6**

John now sees a Lamb with seven horns and seven eyes, standing in the midst of the elders and the living creatures. The Lamb looks as if it had been slain. Many commentators associate this with the sacrificial lamb of Jewish ritual. John the Baptist declared, "Look, the Lamb of God, who takes away the sin of the world!" (John 1:29).

However, several considerations point in another direction. The Greek word used here for lamb (arnion) occurs twenty-nine times in Revelation and only once elsewhere in the New Testament. In verses like John 1:29, the more common word for lamb (amnos) is used. This suggests a special meaning for the word lamb in Revelation.

Far from being a meek animal led to the slaughter (as in Isa. 53:7), the Lamb of Revelation wages a victorious war over his enemies, overcoming them "because he is Lord of lords and King of kings" (17:14). In the last days the mighty of the earth will call out in desperation to be hidden from "the wrath of the Lamb" (6:16). In Jewish apocalyptic literature, the lamb was a symbol of a powerful military leader. Jesus as the Lamb of Revelation is the one who is to return in final combat and lead his people triumphantly to a place of eternal safety (see 19:11-21). His seven horns speak of perfect power and his seven eyes of perfect knowledge.

**7-8**

The Lamb steps forward and takes the scroll from the hand of God. At this moment the angelic hosts fall before the Lamb in worship and praise. In the verses that follow we find a magnificent series of hymns of adoration. Each of the elders has a harp and golden bowls full of incense. The harps are to accompany the songs about to be sung. The golden bowls of incense are "the prayers of the saints." (This is the second place in Revelation where the author interprets his symbolism; the first is 1:20.) The prayers of God's children ascend to God like a fragrant incense.

**9-10**

The elders raise their voices in a new song. In chapter 4 they gave praise to God for his work in creation (v. 11). Now they sing their praise to the Lamb for his work of redemption. In both cases the exclamation, "You are worthy," reflects the customary adulation of the emperor as he passes in triumphal procession.

The Lamb is worthy to open the scroll for three reasons: he was slain, he purchased men for God, and he granted them the authority to reign on earth. He is worthy, not because of his inherent worth or because of any display of personal power, but because he gave himself in death for the Redemption of man. His victory led him to death. His exaltation followed his surrender (see Phil. 2:8-9). It was by means of his death that the Lamb purchased men for God (see 1 Cor. 6:19-20). The scope of his transaction was universal, including men from every nation, tribe, and ethnic group. These are the "other sheep" of which Jesus spoke in John 10:16.

In the Old Testament the Israelites had been promised that God would make them "a kingdom of priests" (Exod. 19:6). The promise is now fulfilled to the church, the eschatological Israel. Its priestly role is to serve God and rule upon the earth. Now believers share in directing the course of human affairs through prayer. In the future they will reign with Christ (see the millennial scene in chapter 20).

**11-12**

John now sees an innumerable multitude of angels

surrounding the throne of God and the inner circle of elders and living creatures. "Ten thousand times ten thousand" is a poetic phrase meaning beyond calculation. It is not a multiplication problem! This great angelic host raises their voices in an anthem of praise to the Lamb who was slain. He is worthy of power, wealth, wisdom, strength, honor, glory, and praise. He has passed through the dark valley of self-sacrifice and died to redeem a "kingdom of priests" (v. 10). In his exaltation he is to be adorned with the attributes he willingly laid aside.

**13-14**

Verse 13 is the climax of the entire scene of heavenly adoration. Every creature *everywhere* (that is the meaning of "in heaven . . . on and under the earth . . . on the sea") joins in a great roar of acclamation that fills the universe with praise and honor to God and to the Lamb. It is grammatically possible that the four living creatures kept saying "Amen"—that is, they responded antiphonally with a great "Amen" after each of the seven attributes proclaimed by the angelic multitude (v. 12) and the four attributes declared by the entire created universe (v. 13). As a fitting finale the elders fall prostrate before the throne and worship both God and the Lamb.

## QUESTIONS

1. How does a scroll differ from an ordinary book?
2. What is the significance of the scroll having writing on both sides?
3. What does the scroll contain?
4. Why did John weep?
5. Explain the two titles: the "Lion of the tribe of

Judah" and the "Root of David."

6.  What does it mean that these titles had been inter-
    preted messianically?
7.  In apocalypticism what did the Lamb represent?
8.  How does Scripture interpret the seven eyes of the
    Lamb? What quality in the Lamb do they signify?
9.  What indication is there in this chapter that God
    hears the prayers of believers?
10. Why is the Lamb worthy to open the scroll? How
    does this explain why no one else was found
    worthy?
11. In what two ways did the death of the Lamb affect
    the future of man?
12. Why did Christ make believers a kingdom of
    priests?
13. What is the largest crowd of people you have ever
    seen? Imagine them all singing praise to God. Does
    this help you to envision the scene of heavenly
    adoration in verses 6-14?
14. What indication is there in verse 13 that the Lamb
    is honored equally with God the Father?
15. In our relationship to God, do you think it would
    be helpful to develop a greater sense of his glory
    and honor? How can you do this?

# REVELATION
# SIX

THE STAGE IS NOW SET, and the eschatological drama is about to begin. John watches as the Lamb himself opens the first of the seven seals. With a voice like thunder, one of the four living creatures calls out, "Come!" Suddenly a white horse appears. The rider holds a bow and is given a crown. He rides forth "as a conqueror bent on conquest."

**1-2**

Many scholars take the rider of the white horse to be Christ. In chapter 19 we again meet a white horse and rider. In that context there is no doubt about his identity—he is "KING OF KINGS AND LORD OF LORDS" (19:16; see also 19:13).

When the two passages are studied side by side, however, it is apparent that the two riders have nothing in common beyond the color of the horses they ride. Since the three horsemen to follow in chapter 6 represent the natural consequences of human sin and aggression (red stands for bloodshed, black for famine, and pale for death), it is better to take our clue from "he rode out as a conqueror bent on conquest" and interpret the white horse as the spirit of military conquest. This retains the close interrelationship between all four horsemen. The interpretation is further strengthened by the fact that in the Old Testament the bow was a symbol of military power (see Hos. 1:5) and in the New Testament the crown (Greek: *stephanos*, victor's wreath) portrays victory.

**3-4**

With the opening of each of the first four seals, the same scenario is enacted. The Lamb removes the seal, and one of the living creatures issues the command to come. The horse that comes out when the second seal is opened is fiery red in color. Its rider is given power to take peace from the earth and cause men to kill one another. This symbolizes the bloodshed that follows the passion to conquer (the white horse and rider). While modern warfare is far more lethal in its destructive power, ancient wars were often more bloody because of person-to-person combat.

Some writers have suggested that if the white horse represents military aggression from without, the red horse may symbolize internal strife and revolution ("men slay each other"). In the thirty-year period before Herod the Great, some one-hundred-thousand persons died in revolutions in Palestine alone. The short sword (Greek: *machaira*, in contrast to *rhomphaia*, large sword, of v. 8) was well suited to this sort of rebellion.

Note that the rider "was given" power to incite the

nations to war. God allows the hostility of man, but he also determines its limits. A strong sense of divine sovereignty runs throughout the Book of Revelation and supplies the basis for confidence that God will bring about the final victory of righteousness over evil.

**5-6**

The third horse to be unleashed is black. Its rider holds a pair of scales in his hand. The black horse represents famine. In ancient days when conquering armies lived off the lands they had just overrun, the commodities left behind would be exceedingly scarce. The scales picture the careful weighing out of grain in a time of famine. The voice John hears says that for a day's wages a man is to receive only enough wheat for himself or enough of the less nutritious barley for three.

The prohibition against damaging the oil and wine has been interpreted in many ways. The most satisfactory is that it is a limit set upon the famine. Since the roots of the olive tree and the grape vine go deep into the soil, a drought that would devastate the grain would not seriously affect the oil and wine. God is allowing the famine but limiting its extent.

**7-8**

The fourth horse is pale in color (like a corpse or the face of a person struck with terror). Its rider is death, and Hades is his inseparable companion. To them is given the power to kill with what the prophet Ezekiel calls "my four dreadful judgments"—sword and famine and wild beasts and plague (see Ezek. 14: 21). These plagues for the most part overlap with the consequences of the previous horsemen. Death by wild beasts would be expected as an aftermath of war that left many who had fallen unattended.

The four horsemen of the Apocalypse symbolize the kind of limited and preliminary judgment that follows naturally from the aggressive nature of man. It is allowed by God as a consequence of man's sin. It is not the direct outpouring of divine wrath. Not until the seventh seal is removed and the scroll is actually opened do we enter into the final stage that witnesses the righteous retribution of God upon all the evil of the world.

**9-10**

Revelation contains three series of plagues—seals, trumpets, and bowls, each of which is numbered one through seven. Each series is divided into an initial four, which bear close resemblance to one another, and an additional three. Thus after the four horsemen, the sequence changes. With the opening of the fifth seal, we find a group of martyrs calling out for judgment upon the wicked and the vindication of their faith.

The altar in John's vision seems to be in heaven. The martyrs are those whose lives have been sacrificed because of the testimony they have maintained. The fact that they are "under the altar" may reflect the Old Testament practice of pouring sacrificial blood at the altar's base (see Lev. 4:7). Like Antipas of Pergamum (2:13), they remained true even at the cost of their lives.

The martyrs' plea for judgment upon "the inhabitants of the earth" (a designation for mankind in his hostility to God) should not be taken in the sense of personal revenge. Throughout the Old Testament, especially in the Psalms, there is a profound concern for the reputation and honor of God. For God's people to suffer shame is for God to appear powerless against his enemies. Hence the concern that the faithful be vindicated so God's name is not held in dishonor. Since God is sovereign, holy, and true, he must of necessity avenge the death of the faithful. The only question is when.

**11**

The martyrs are given white robes, symbolic of the

righteousness that is now theirs. They are to wait a little longer until the complete number of fellow martyrs is reached. When all who are to sacrifice their lives as martyrs have been put to death, then God will bring history to a close and vindicate believers in a final judgment.

**12-14**

When the sixth seal is opened, the entire universe is thrown into turmoil. Not only does a great earthquake alter the face of the earth ("every mountain and island was removed from its place"), but sun and moon are darkened and stars fall to the earth. To ancients who viewed the orderly universe as an indication of God's sovereign control, these great cataclysmic events would constitute a grim announcement that the end had come. In the Old Testament the earthquake often heralded a divine visitation. When God came down on Mount Sinai, "the whole mountain trembled violently" (Exod. 19:18; see also Isa. 2:19).

Since apocalyptic writing is characterized by dramatic images and striking figures of speech, this portrayal of a universe in dissolution is not to be taken with rigid literalism. The language is similar to the poetic descriptions in the Old Testament of the "mountains [skipping] like lambs" (Ps. 114:4) and the "trees of the field [clapping] their hands" (Isa. 55:12). But neither should the passage be allegorized so as to represent nothing more than upheavals in the social and political world. It is an apocalyptic portrayal of the end of history when this world as we know it gives way to the next.

**15-17**

The description continues with a dramatic presentation of the effects of the cosmic disturbances on mankind. Kings, princes, generals, the rich and powerful, slave and free, all flee to caves in the mountains. Yet even there security eludes them. Rather than face the wrath of the Lamb, they cry out to the mountains and rocks to fall on them. With the approach of the end and the realization that they are about to face the wrath of God, the hearts of men are gripped by terror. The rocks and mountains that move at God's command cannot provide a hiding place. Those who have spurned the love of God must now reap his intense hatred for all that is evil and contrary to his holy will. The concept of a wrathful Lamb is not paradoxical when we remember that the Lamb in Revelation is a messianic warrior, not a meek sacrificial animal.

The sixth seal has brought us to the beginning of the end. In one sense it goes beyond itself and portrays a setting described more fully in the initial trumpets and the first four bowls. Some writers find a repetition or recapitulation in the three numbered series. Careful study, however, reveals not a carefully designed scheme of recapitulation but a free use of common apocalyptic symbols. As the end approaches, there is an accompanying increase in the intensity of distress. Revelation is not prewritten, historical narrative but a highly impressionistic portrayal of the end of the age, the return of Christ, the judgment of evil, and the eternal blessedness of the righteous.

## QUESTIONS

1. What do the white horse and rider symbolize? Which clause in verse 2 provides the clue?
2. What is symbolized by the bow and the crown?
3. What is symbolized by the fiery-red horse?
4. To what extent has history been shaped by the first two horsemen?

5. Why did famine so often follow war in ancient days?

6. What is meant by the restriction against damaging the oil and wine?

7. How does this restriction illustrate the sovereignty of God?

8. What is taught by the fact that death and Hades are "given power" to kill?

9. Who are the ones "under the altar"?

10. Why do they ask God to avenge their deaths?

11. What is the necessary connection between God as "sovereign . . . holy and true" and the judgment of evil men?

12. How would you answer the charge that the martyrs' attitude was less than Christian?

13. Why were the martyrs told to wait a little longer?

14. What do the cosmic disturbances of the sixth seal represent?

15. On what basis are we permitted to interpret the great upheavals (vv. 12-14) in a less than literal fashion?

16. In the last days why will unbelieving men call for the rocks and mountains to fall on them?

17. How can God, who is love, have wrath?

# REVELATION
# SEVEN

CHAPTER SEVEN CONSISTS of two visions that fall between the opening of the sixth and seventh seals. A
similar parenthesis is found between the sixth and seventh trumpets (10:1—11:13). The strategic placement of
these interludes creates a sense of heightened expectancy as the drama of the last days moves toward its
climax.

**1**

Verses 1-8 describe the sealing of the 144,000.

John sees four angels standing at the four corners of
the earth, restraining the four winds of destruction. The
description is highly metaphorical. Reference to the
"four corners of the earth" is not intended to imply that

the earth is square (or rectangular). We still speak of the "four corners" of the earth. This part of the vision shows that the destructive winds of nature (for instance, the sirocco, a searing wind from the desert that left withered vegetation in its wake) are being restrained by heavenly beings.

**2-3**

Then from the east (perhaps a reference to Palestine) comes another angel bearing the seal of the living God. He orders the four angels not to harm the land, sea, or trees until the servants of God are sealed on the forehead.

The seal was probably a signet ring used by ancient dignitaries to protect the contents of official documents. (A scroll would be closed with a small disk of molten wax into which the distinctive seal of the sender was pressed.) From Revelation 14:1 we learn that the mark upon the foreheads of God's servants consisted of the names of the Lamb and of God the Father. The purpose of sealing the 144,000 was to protect that last generation of believers, who are about to enter the final tumultuous days before the end. The protection is not physical (the two witnesses in chapter 11 are killed by the beast) but spiritual. God insures that the final demonic assault of Satan will be unable to affect the destiny of his people.

It is worth noting that it is the seal of the *living* God. Over against the false and impotent gods of heathendom, the God of the Apocalypse is living and therefore able to grant perfect protection to those who bear his name.

**4-8**

John does not witness the sealing; he only hears that 144,000 have been sealed. From each of the twelve tribes of Israel 12,000 are sealed. But who, in fact, are the 144,000?

Answers abound. Some think that they constitute a select group of martyrs. Yet according to chapter 13:15 we learn that *all*, not a chosen few, who do not worship the image of the beast are killed. The careful listing of 12,000 from each tribe suggests completeness rather than selectivity.

Others feel that the 144,000 are literal Jews chosen from the various tribes of the reconstituted nation of Israel. Apart from the obvious historical problem that the ten northern tribes disappeared in Assyria and the other two lost their national identity with the fall of Jerusalem, several irregularities exist in Revelation's listing of the tribes. It is Judah, rather than Reuben (the oldest son of Jacob), who heads the list. Both Joseph and his son Manasseh are listed, although the latter would be included with his father. And we would expect Manasseh's brother Ephraim to be listed if the tribe of Joseph is to be divided. Finally, the tribe of Dan is omitted.

These irregularities suggest that we are not to take the list as a prophetic genealogical chart. The order of the tribes is without significance. The number 144,000 is symbolic: it squares the number of the tribes of Israel (12 × 12 = 144) and multiplies the sum by 1,000. This is a graphic way of representing the number of faithful believers who will enter the dark days before the end.

They are sealed to identify them as belonging to God and to protect them from the wrath of Satan. Referring to the church as the tribes of Israel comes from the New Testament teaching that the church is the "Israel of God" (Gal. 6:16; cf. Matt. 19:28; James 1:1; 1 Pet. 2:9).
**9-10**

The two visions of chapter 7 stand in sharp contrast. In the first, John saw 144,000 about to enter a period of hostility before the end. In the second, we meet an innumerable multitude "who have come out of the great tribulation" (v. 14) and surround the throne of heaven, praising God and the Lamb. The purpose of the second vision is to draw back the curtain of eternity and encourage believers by revealing the blessedness awaiting them in the eternal state.

The great multitude around the throne includes people from every sector of the human race. Every nation, tribe, people, and language is represented. Their white robes speak of righteousness and the palm branches they hold mark the occasion as one of festive joy. Their song is the joyous proclamation that their deliverance has been effected by God and by the Lamb. It was the will of God that they be saved, and this salvation was carried out by the death of the Lamb (see 5: 9).

**11-12**

Around the innumerable multitude of saints is an equally great host of angels (see 5:11). They fall on their faces in worship of God and join their voices in a sevenfold doxology. During his earthly ministry Jesus had said, "There is rejoicing in the presence of the angels of God over one sinner who repents" (Luke 15:10). Imagine the scene in heaven when *all* repentant sinners stand redeemed before the throne of God!

The first amen of verse 12 may be a response to the praise of the multitude in verse 10. Or it may, with the second amen, bracket the angels' own doxology. Praise, glory, wisdom, thanks, honor, power, and strength all belong to God for ever and ever. To acknowledge his worth is the privilege of the angelic hosts.

**13-14**

At this point, one of the elders asks John about the white-robed multitude. Who are they and where did they come from? John answers, "Sir, you know" (see Zech. 4: 5 for the same question-and-answer format to introduce the explanation of a vision). The elder then indicates that the multitude are those who have come out of the great tribulation.

Throughout history the people of God have often suffered for their faith. "In this world you will have trouble" promised Jesus (John 16:33). "Everyone who wants to live a godly life in Christ Jesus will be persecuted" taught Paul (2 Tim. 3:12). This continuing antagonism against believers will reach its highest pitch in that final period of turmoil before the end. It will thus become the *great* tribulation.

The multitude before the throne have washed their robes and made them white in the blood of the Lamb. The garments of all men have been stained with sin (see Rom. 3:23). They can be cleansed only by an active faith in the redeeming power of the death of Christ. In John's language they are washed white in the blood of the Lamb (see Isa. 1:18). The act of washing is not a meritorious act on the part of man—something he does to earn forgiveness. It is a way of portraying faith.

**15-17**

Since the innumerable host has remained faithful in the period of final testing, they are now rewarded by being in the presence of God and ready to serve him unceasingly. God, in turn, spreads his tent over them to shelter and protect them from all harm. This imagery would remind John's readers of the tabernacle in the wilderness and God's protection of Israel by means of a pillar of cloud by day and fire by night (Exod. 13:21-22). Never again will they hunger or thirst. Beyond the obvious physical reference is the promise that their deepest longings for spiritual wholeness will be satisfied in the eternal state. To a people accustomed to the scorching heat of the Near East, the promise of relief from the sun would be welcomed.

## WHAT ARE WE WAITING FOR?

The white-robed multitude is pictured as a flock of sheep with the infinite good fortune of having the Lamb as their shepherd (see John 10:1-30). This metaphor reaches back into Old Testament times. The psalmist sang, "The Lord is my shepherd, I shall lack nothing" (Ps. 23:1), and Isaiah declared of God, "He tends his flock like a shepherd" (Isa. 40:11). Specifically, the Lamb will lead them to springs of living water. Eternal refreshment is in store for those who follow Christ. And God will wipe away every tear from their eyes. There will be no sorrow in heaven—only tears left over from the travail of life on earth. These God will quickly remove.

Verses 15-19 look forward to that time of eternal joy, which awaits the church when it has passed through the great tribulation. This description of heavenly comfort and joy is perhaps the greatest portrayal of eternal bliss to be found anywhere in religious literature.

## QUESTIONS

1.  How would you answer the argument that the reference in verse 1 to the "four corners of the earth" reveals that the ancients believed in a square earth?
2.  What is the "seal of the living God"?
3.  Does the sealing protect the servants of God from physical harm? What is the basis for your answer?
4.  Who are the 144,000?
5.  List and explain the three irregularities in the listing of the twelve tribes.
6.  What is the "Israel of God" in the New Testament? What does this imply about the relationship between the two testaments?

7. Does the second vision of the chapter relate to a time before or after the return of Christ? Explain.
8. Who are those in white robes?
9. What is the great tribulation?
10. What does the second vision teach about whether or not the church will be raptured before the tribulation?
11. In verses 15-17, the elder describes the blessings of heaven in terms especially meaningful for those living in first-century Palestine. What terms could be used in the twentieth century to convey the same impact?
12. How can you explain tears in heaven?

# REVELATION
# EIGHT

THE PARENTHETICAL VISIONS of chapter 7 are over. The Lamb now resumes his role as the one who is opening the seven-sealed scroll.

**1**

When he removes the seventh and last seal, we might expect one great final upheaval as a proper climax to the series of catastrophes, ranging from war to cosmic disturbances. Instead, there is silence. No sound is heard in heaven for about half an hour. Silence is often more dramatic than sound. As a prelude to all that follows it is entirely appropriate at this moment.

**2-5**

The activity described here apparently takes place during the half hour of silence. John sees seven angels standing before God. Each is given a trumpet. The trumpet was used extensively in Old Testament times for a variety of purposes. It served, for example, to gather the people of Israel (Num. 10: 2-3), to celebrate sacred feasts (Num. 10:10), and in connection with the coronation of kings (1 Kings 1: 34). In Revelation, however, the trumpets announce the wrath of God. The first four trumpet blasts herald physical calamities, the next two bring demonic plagues, and the last proclaims the demise of all worldly systems.

Scholars are divided on the relationship between the three series of numbered visions (seals, trumpets, and bowls). One common view is that they follow each other in chronological sequence, with the last unit of each series becoming the sevenfold series to follow. That is, the seven trumpets *are* the seventh seal, and the seven bowls *are* the seventh trumpet. Since the seven bowls are all contained in the seventh trumpet and the seven trumpets are all part of the seventh seal, it may be said that both series of plagues are a part of the opening of the seventh seal. Diagrammed, it would look like this:

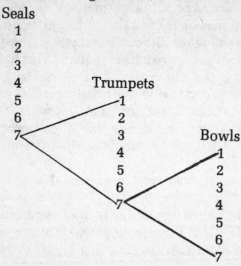

# WHAT ARE WE WAITING FOR?

A second approach is called recapitulation. In this scheme, the three series are chronologically parallel, and each brings us to the close of history. The same ground is covered by each series.

| Seals | 1 | 2 | 3 | 4 | 5 | 6 | 7 |
|---|---|---|---|---|---|---|---|
| Trumpets | 1 | 2 | 3 | 4 | 5 | 6 | 7 |
| Bowls | 1 | 2 | 3 | 4 | 5 | 6 | 7 |

My position is that neither scheme is totally accurate. From a strictly literary standpoint, the first approach represents the progression of the text. The recapitulation approach answers the question raised by the close parallelism between the first four trumpets and the first four bowls (plagues fall on earth, sea, rivers, and streams; sun, moon, and stars—compare 8:7-12 with 16:2-8). While the numbered visions present a rather clear literary progression, it is less certain that we are to understand a corresponding *chronological* development. What is clear is that as the end approaches the intensity of the plagues increases correspondingly.

Now another angel approaches the altar. In his hand is a golden censer (or fire pan). The incense he burns before the altar is mingled with believers' prayers, which ascend to God. (Some hold that the incense is the prayers of the saints.) God is mindful of the prayers of his children, which arise unceasingly before the heavenly throne.

The censer, an implement of ceremonial worship, is now put to a different use. It is filled with fire from the altar and hurled upon the earth. It would appear that prayer has moved God to act in judgment. The prayers of the martyrs in chapter 6 are now beginning to be answered. The angel's hurling fire upon the earth is accompanied by lightning, thunder, and an earthquake—common symbols of the divine presence (see Exod. 19:16—20:21).

**6-9**

Against this background, the seven angels prepare to sound their trumpets. At the sound of the first, hail and fire mixed with blood are hurled upon the earth. It is characteristic of John to draw his imagery from existing sources. Both the Old Testament and intertestamental apocalyptic literature supply his rhetorical needs. For example, in Exodus 9:23-25, God rained hail and flashing fire upon the land of Egypt. In the *Sibylline Oracles* (a mixture of Jewish and Christian prophetic utterances claiming to have originated with Greek sibyls or fortune-tellers), one of the signs of the last days is a rain of fire and blood.

The author of Revelation, however, is not bound by his sources. With sovereign freedom he blends together a kaleidoscope of images, in order to portray a message that bears no essential relationship to the original contexts of its literary sources. Of course, these are still images that John *saw*. Although God was responsible for the visions, they find expression in the specific terms of John's own religious culture and vocabulary.

As a result of the fire, a third of the earth was burned up, also a third of the trees and all the green grass. While the first four seals portrayed the inevitable consequences of human sin, the trumpets introduce direct divine intervention in judgment. Yet this judgment is not complete. Always it is *one-third* of everything that is affected (the fraction occurs twelve times in verses 7-12). From chapter 9:20-21 we infer that the trumpets are warnings intended to call men to repentance.

When the second angel sounds his trumpet, something like a blazing mountain is thrown into the sea. A third of the sea turns to blood, and a third of the sea creatures and ships are destroyed. Some writers note that less than twenty years before John wrote Revelation, Vesuvius erupted and buried Pompeii in molten lava. It is impossible to determine whether this cataclysm furnished the imagery for John's burning mountain. The destruction is serious (one-third) but not complete.

**10-12**

At the command of the third trumpet, a blazing star falls on a third of the rivers and streams, turning them bitter and bringing about the death of many people. Even more terrifying are the results of the fourth trumpet. Blackness settles over the earth for a third of the day and a third of the night. Sun, moon, and stars are blackened.

Do not try to press these details into some sort of prosaic scheme. As the trumpets are blown one by one, God begins to disrupt the orderly processes of nature as a warning and prelude to the complete disaster about to come. Cosmic disturbances such as hail, bloody fire, blazing mountains, falling stars, and darkness are warnings intended to move wicked men to repentance.

In the first-century world they would strike terror in the heart of man. But even terror will not deter man from his idolatry and shameful life (see 9:20-21). Neither God's kindness (Rom. 2:4) nor his severity is able to alter the conduct of man in rebellion against God. His destiny is determined by his willful resistance to all divine overtures.

**13**

The seven trumpets are divided into groups of four and three (as with the four horsemen of 6:1-8 and the three seals that follow). The first four trumpets call forth plagues upon nature, which affect man indirectly. The remaining plagues are demonic forces, falling directly upon man. They are introduced by a bird of prey, either an eagle or a vulture, hovering overhead and screeching, "Woe! Woe! Woe to the inhabitants of the earth."

The plagues that follow do not fall upon the church but upon pagan society. In chapter 9 the scorpions are to harm "only those people who did not have the seal of God on their foreheads" (9:4). Although believers in the last days will suffer the abuse of wicked men (as they always have—see John 16:33; 2 Tim. 3:12), the wrath of God will never fall on them.

It is only when *tribulation* is defined as the direct outpouring of God's wrath that it can be said that the church does not go through the tribulation. The church always was and always will (until the Second Coming) be subject to the hostility of the world.


## QUESTIONS

1.  What is the significance of the silence in heaven when the seventh seal is opened?
2.  For what purpose are trumpets used in Revelation?
3.  Explain the two basic interpretations of the relationship between the seals, trumpets, and bowls.
4.  In what sense can the prayers of God's people be likened to incense?
5.  On what basis does the commentary hold that thunder and lightning are symbols of divine visitation?
6.  Is "fire mixed with blood" to be taken literally, or is it descriptive in a symbolic sense? Explain.
7.  What is the significance of the recurring mention of one-third?

8. To what extent is John bound to the sources of his images?
9. Since God is responsible for John's vision, why do commentators refer to Old Testament or apocalyptic backgrounds for the images used?
10. Why is verse 12 not describing an eclipse?
11. What seems to be the purpose of the trumpet plagues?
12. How do the first four trumpet plagues differ from those that follow?

# REVELATION
# NINE

IT ONLY TOOK SIX VERSES for John to set forth the first
four trumpet plagues. Now he is going to devote an
entire chapter to the next two, which indicates the seriousness of the woes to follow.

**1-6**

At the sound of the fifth trumpet, a star falls to the
earth. The star is quite obviously a person, because he
takes a key and opens the abyss. Out billow dense
clouds of smoke that blot out the sun and darken the sky.
The abyss is a great subterranean chasm inhabited by all
manner of evil beings—the scorpion centaurs who torture men, their demonic King Abaddon (v. 11), and the
cruel beast of chapter 11, who assaults and murders the
two witnesses.

## WHAT ARE WE WAITING FOR?

The locusts, swarming out of the abyss and emerging from the smoke, are given the scorpion's power to torture but not to kill. In the Old Testament, the locust served as a symbol of devastation and destruction. The prophet Joel pictured the dark side of the coming day of the Lord by means of a great plague of locusts (Joel 1:2—2:11).

The demonic locusts of Revelation, however, do not harm the vegetation. Rather, they inflict their torture upon those inhabitants of the land who do not bear the seal of God upon their foreheads. This is the strongest possible evidence that believers will never be subjected to the evil powers of the underworld. They may be buffeted by the opposition of man, but they are sealed against the demonic (see Rev. 7:1-8; also the protection given the children of Israel from the first Egyptian plagues, Exod. 8:22; 9:4, 26; etc.).

The locusts are allowed to torment man for a period of five months. This period of time probably stems from the life expectancy of the locust. It represents a limited period of torment during which man may still repent of his wickedness (vv. 20-21). In one of the most vivid presentations of human distress, we learn that during those days men will seek death and not find it; they will long to die, but death will elude them. The issues at stake in the age-long conflict between God and Satan are deadly serious. To choose wickedness is a decision that will lead to unmitigated suffering.

**7-12**

The locusts are described as horses prepared for battle. The similarity between the head of a locust and a horse's head has often been noticed. In fact, the German word for locust is *Heupferd* (hay horse). The description of the demonic locusts is bizarre in the extreme. Their faces are like human faces. They wear something like crowns of gold. They are covered with long hair like that of a woman, and their teeth are like a lion's. The picture that emerges combines human intelligence and animal cruelty. It is unnatural and frightening.

The locusts are protected by breastplates of iron. Their flight sounds like a multitude of chariots rushing into battle. One of the nonbiblical Jewish books tells of elephants who wore coats of mail and made a terrific din as they charged the enemy. As we learned earlier, the locusts have scorpionlike tails and the power to inflict pain for five months.

They also have a king. His name in Hebrew is Abaddon, the destroyer. In case the reader fails to grasp the significance of the Hebrew name, John adds the Greek equivalent, Apollyon. As king of the demonic locusts, his mission is to destroy. Some find here a cryptic reference to the practice of certain Roman emperors who regarded themselves as an incarnation of the god Apollo. The play on words (Apollyon/Apollo) would be a subtle way of saying that the emperor of Rome was in fact the king of the underworld and all its destructive forces.

Commentators who understand the bulk of Revelation as describing life in the present age normally interpret the locusts as a sort of personification of evil. Hair "like women's hair" is said to symbolize the seductive nature of evil. But hairy locusts with lion's teeth and scorpion's tails are not most people's idea of a seductive creature! Although certain features in this portrayal may represent truths that have found expression from time to time in human history, I believe the locust plague is an eschatological event. It belongs to the end of time.

The last three trumpet plagues are named the three woes. Verse 12 announces that the terrifying horde of demonic locusts is only the first woe. Two more will follow. The plight of unrepentant man will continue from bad to worse as the end approaches.

**13-19**

When the sixth angel blows his trumpet, John hears a voice from the golden altar. It is helpful to remember that the martyrs in chapter 6 who called out for vindication were "under the altar." Further, the prayers of the saints in chapter 8 arose from "the golden altar before the throne" (v. 3). The point is that the prayers of God's children play an active role in bringing about the close of history. In Jesus' sermon about the last days, he indicated that the end would come only after the gospel of the Kingdom of God has been preached throughout the entire world (Matt. 24:14).

The voice from the altar orders the sixth angel to release the four angels who are bound at the great river Euphrates. The Euphrates was the longest river in western Asia (almost eighteen-hundred miles) and marked the eastern boundary of Israel, following the conquests of David (2 Sam. 8:3; 1 Kings 4:24).

The four angels are apparently in charge of the demonic cavalry that is about to ride across the earth killing a third of mankind. (The word *angel* is often used in secular sources for supernatural beings connected with the underworld.) They have been kept ready for this specific moment in time. Note the emphasis on year, month, day, and hour. God is in control and will release the forces of destruction when he decides the time is exactly right.

The mission of the locusts is to torment (v. 5). The mission of the cavalry is to kill (v. 15). As each new plague brings man closer to the end, the intensity of punishment increases. Apparently even the severest of plagues fails to bring about repentance (vv. 20-21).

The mounted troops released by the four angels are beyond calculation. The figure "two hundred million" is not to be taken as an actual number. The Greek says, "a double-myriad of myriads." We might translate, "countless thousands" (a myriad is 10,000). What we need to sense is how absolutely terrifying the sight would be. It would instantly paralyze even the bravest with fear and demoralize all potential opposition.

All we are told about the riders is that they wear multicolored breastplates (they did not play an active role in carrying out the plague). The colors (fiery red, dark blue, sulfur yellow) match the fire, smoke, and sulfur that come out of the mouths of the horses.

The horses are grotesque. They have lionlike heads with mouths that breathe out fire and smoke. Their tails are like snakes with heads that inflict injury. Picture an enormous cavalry of fire-breathing monsters sweeping over the land. Add to it their demonic origin and their power to kill, and you will sense the terrifying reality of the second woe. The great horde moving relentlessly across the face of earth leaves a third of mankind dead.

**20-21**

The final verses of chapter 9 are a sad commentary on human nature. One would think that a plague of demonic horses killing one out of every three persons would bring the survivors to their senses. But those who were not killed in the three plagues of fire, smoke, and sulfur did not repent of their idolatry. They continued to worship demons and dumb idols they had crafted of wood, metal, and stone. Further, they did not repent of their heathen practices of murder, sorcery, immorality, and theft. When people willfully turn from the knowledge of God, they soon pass the point of no return along a road that leads downward into idolatry and immorality (see Rom. 1:18-32).

# WHAT ARE WE WAITING FOR?

The theme of idolatry is prominent in Jewish litera-ture. Not until the seventy years of Babylonian captivity did the Israelites overcome their persistent tendency to lapse into pagan worship. On Mount Carmel, for in-stance, the prophet Elijah laid out the options for Israel: "If the Lord is God, follow him; but if Baal is God, follow him" (1 Kings 18: 21). In the New Testament Paul taught that to offer sacrifice to an idol was to sacrifice to de-mons (1 Cor. 10: 20). At the end of time, men will still choose to honor and worship the demons that inflict suffering and death. Such is the perverse nature of man who refuses to acknowledge the lordship of Christ.

It is interesting to note that three of the four vices listed in the final verse of the chapter are prohibited in the Ten Commandments. The fourth (magic arts, or witchcraft) is listed by Paul as a work of the flesh (Gal. 5: 20), which ultimately leads to the fiery lake of burning sulfur (Rev. 21: 8).

## QUESTIONS

1. On what basis is it correct to say that the star of verses 1-2 is a person? What does this tell you about interpretation of apocalyptic literature?
2. What is the abyss?
3. Why will the locust plague not affect the believers who are alive at that time?
4. What do the five months of verse 5 stand for?
5. Why are those who wish to die during the locust plague unable to do so?
6. What qualities are suggested by the description of the demonic locusts (vv. 7-10)?
7. Who is the king of the locusts? What do his names mean?

8. What is the significance of the fact that the request to unloose the angels of destruction comes from a voice connected with the golden altar?
9. Is 200 million to be taken as a specific number? Why or why not?
10. How did the demonic cavalry kill?
11. Why do you suppose those who escaped death during the cavalry plague refused to repent?
12. Why do people worship idols?
13. Why is there a natural connection between misplaced worship (v. 20) and such sins as violence and sex (v. 21)?

# REVELATION
# TEN

THERE WAS AN interlude of two related visions between the sixth and seventh seal (7:1-8; 9-17). Now we encounter a similar parenthesis between the sixth and seventh trumpet (10:1-11; 11:1-13). From a literary standpoint the interludes are dramatic pauses that heighten the sense of expectancy as the end approaches. In addition, the two visions that follow the sixth trumpet answer the questions "How long until the end?" and "What will happen to the church during this troubled period?"

**1-4**

At the beginning of chapter 4, John was summoned from earth to heaven, and he saw the subsequent visions from that perspective. Now he is once again on earth (he sees an angel "coming down from heaven," v. 1). The mighty angel who descends is described in terms that reflect his Old Testament background.

In Psalm 104:3 God is said to make the clouds his chariot. The rainbow was a sign of God's covenant with man that the earth would never again be destroyed by water (Gen. 9:8-17). When Moses came from the presence of God on Mount Sinai, his face shone with such radiance that he had to wear a veil (Exod. 34:29-35).

In this chapter of Revelation, the angel's legs like fiery pillars would recall the pillars of fire and cloud that guided (Exod. 13:21-22) and gave protection (Exod. 14:19-24) to the children of Israel as they fled from the armies of Pharaoh during the Exodus.

I mention these Old Testament parallels to show that visions, like dreams, draw upon the wide range of experiences and information that have become part of the writer. In the same way that Paul's writing reflects a vocabulary and style different from Luke's (yet it is God who speaks through both), so the visions of John are cast in terminology and images that were dominant in his spiritual background and understanding.

The mighty angel plants one foot on the sea and the other on the land. This stance is probably intended to indicate his tremendous size, although some find here a reference to universal sovereignty (land and sea). In his hand is a little scroll. In contrast to the seven-sealed scroll of chapter 4, whose content could be known only after each seal was removed, the little scroll lay open to be read immediately.

The angel gives a great shout like the roar of a lion, and the seven thunders respond. Exactly who the seven thunders are is not known. Nor is there any indication of what they said. All we know is that John was about to write it down when he was told by a voice from heaven to seal up what was said and not record it. Some think that the thunder may have given another series of warning plagues, but since man had not repented after the extreme distress caused by the earlier plagues, there would be no reason to go through another series. While this is obviously conjecture, it is not out of harmony with what we might expect.

One additional point needs to be made. When the seven thunders speak, John prepares to write down what they say. It appears that during his visionary experiences the apostle kept notes, which make up the Book of Revelation. This would account for the vivid descriptions that characterize the book. Revelation is not the literary product of an exiled eccentric bent on creating an exciting drama, but the eyewitness account of a prophet who in the Spirit (1:10; 4:2) described what he actually saw.

5-7

The mighty angel who stands astride the land and sea raises his right hand to heaven and swears by the one who lives forever that the end of this age will take place without further delay. In ancient days (as well as today) raising the right hand was part of taking an oath. In Deuteronomy God himself is pictured as lifting his hand to heaven and swearing that he will take vengeance on his enemies (Deut. 32:40).

The description of God as the one who lives for ever and ever would encourage the early Christians facing the prospects of martyrdom. Man may take life, but God is beyond the threat of death and supplies eternal life to the faithful. He is also creator. As the one who created all things out of nothing (Heb. 11:3), he is able to carry through what he began.

Man has always been interested in the question of

how long it will be until the end. There have been those in every generation convinced that they were living in the last few moments of history. As the end seems to draw near, concern for its actual arrival increases. The martyrs under the fifth seal asked, "How long, Sovereign Lord . . . until you judge the inhabitants of the earth and avenge our blood?" (6:10).

The immediate answer was to wait (6:11), but now the mighty angel can declare that there will no longer be any delay. The warning plagues have gone out, and man has refused to repent. Whatever was intended by the seven thunders has been canceled. From this point forward, nothing can stop the inexorable flow of events that will bring history to its close. All restraint is to be removed, and man will enter the final dark hours of Satan's great wrath (12:12, 17).

During the period of time introduced by the trumpet blast of the seventh angel, the mystery of God is to be brought to completion. A "mystery" in biblical thought is a truth that was formerly hidden but is now made clear by revelation. Mysteries often have an eschatological coloring. For instance, the mystery of 1 Corinthians 15:51, 52 (a change from mortality to immortality) takes place when Christ returns. The "mystery of God" that is to be accomplished in the day of the seventh trumpet is the completion of God's great redemptive mission, which was purposed in creation and made possible by the work of the Lamb (5:9-10). Note that God has determined the overthrow of evil from the very first. His purpose to redeem runs throughout history, and he had announced it to his prophets. As Amos wrote, "Surely the Sovereign Lord does nothing without revealing his plan to his servants the prophets" (Amos 3:7).

**8-11**

Once again the voice from heaven speaks. John is told

to take the open scroll from the hand of the angel, who is robed in a cloud with a rainbow above his head, a face like the sun, and legs like fiery pillars, standing astride land and sea. Nothing short of a command from heaven would move the seer to approach the supernatural colossus and take a scroll from his hand.

John obeys the heavenly voice and takes the scroll. He is then told to eat it. What follows is given as a riddle. The scroll will be as sweet as honey in the mouth but turn the stomach sour. John eats the scroll and finds this is true. What does this strange experience mean?

To eat the scroll means to digest thoroughly its content. The psalmist wrote that God's words were sweet to his taste, sweeter than honey to his mouth (Ps. 119:103). Jeremiah reports that upon finding God's words he "ate them," and they became the delight of his heart (Jer. 15:16).

Writers differ quite a bit about what is intended by the little scroll. I believe it is a message for the believing church and is found in the first thirteen verses of the following chapter (11:1-13). In this section we will learn that after the witnessing church has completed its testimony, the Christians will be put to death. As the great scroll of chapter 5 dealt with the destiny of all mankind, the little scroll reveals the lot of the faithful during the final period of satanic opposition. The scroll is sweet to the taste, because there will be no more delay in bringing to a close God's eternal purpose to redeem mankind. It will be sour in the stomach, because it will involve a time of fierce opposition and much sorrow.

In verse 11 John is told that he must prophesy again about the destiny of mankind as a whole. In the seals and the trumpets, we learned of judgments against the ungodly. After the interlude of 10:1—11:14 (the church in the world during the final days), John will return to the theme of God's judgment of the wicked (11:15 and following).

There is a sense of divine compulsion in the fact that John must prophesy again. His task is not over until he has carried through to the very end. There is much that remains before Satan and his emissaries are put away forever, and righteousness dwells in a renovated heaven and earth. Until the revelation is complete, John must continue to prophesy.

## QUESTIONS

1. Describe the mighty angel coming down from heaven. Why is he described in Old Testament phrases?
2. Of what would the angel's legs like fiery pillars remind a Jewish reader?
3. In what ways is the little scroll of this chapter unlike the scroll of destiny in chapter 5?
4. What is a probable answer to the question of what the seven thunders may have said?
5. Why was John told not to write this?
6. Why did the mighty angel raise his hand?
7. In this context what is the significance of God being described as living for ever and ever?
8. What is the significance of God being described as having created all things?
9. What delays have there been in Revelation, and what apparently was the reason?
10. What is the "mystery of God" that will be accomplished in the final days?
11. Why would John have to be encouraged to approach the angel? Can you picture yourself in a similar situation? What would be your reaction?

12. What does it mean to "eat" a scroll?
13. What section of Revelation comprises the little scroll?
14. Why is the little scroll sweet as honey in the mouth?
15. Why is it sour in the stomach?
16. Would you be pleased to learn that we are about to enter the final stage of human history? In what ways would this be sweet? In what ways sour?
17. The additional prophesying mentioned in 10:11 begins at what point in the Book of Revelation?

# REVELATION
# ELEVEN

THE FIRST THIRTEEN VERSES of chapter 11 constitute the message of the little scroll, which was sweet in the mouth but sour in the stomach. They deal with the fate of the witnessing church during the final period of hostility before the end. Obviously this requires a symbolic interpretation. We need to remember that if we interpret symbols in a literal fashion we misinterpret the intended meaning.

Furthermore, a great number of words operate on several levels of meaning. The Alamo was a Franciscan mission at San Antonio. But in the slogan, "Remember the Alamo," we are not expected to recall the physical construction of the fort. We are to remember the courage of the Texans who held out bravely for a while, but in the end were massacred by Mexican troops. In this context,

*Alamo* is to be understood as a symbol of bravery in battle.

It is crucial to remember that wherever the context calls for interpretation on a symbolic level, a literal interpretation would be a misinterpretation. Literalness must never be *automatically* equated with accuracy or truthfulness. For instance, in the section that follows, we will discover that the temple is the New Testament church.

### 1-2

John is given a reed and told to measure the temple of God but not the outer court. He is to count the worshipers. The outer court is to be left unmeasured, because it has been given over to the Gentiles who will trample the holy city for forty-two months. What does all this mean?

The temple is the church, the people of God (see 1 Cor. 3:16-17; Eph. 2:19-22). To measure the temple means to preserve it. God's people are to be protected in the coming catastrophe (compare the sealing of the faithful in 7:1-8).

Yet the outer court is to be trampled underfoot. In another sense the church is to be subject to severe opposition and suffering. How do these two ideas fit together? In the last days the church will suffer persecution, but it will be provided spiritual sanctuary against the assaults of Satan. Its protection is against *spiritual* danger. Martyrdom has always been a potential hazard of following Christ in a godless world, but Satan cannot harm spiritually those who have made a genuine commitment to Christ.

The forty-two months during which the holy city (the church) is trampled underfoot by pagan forces corresponds to the 1,260 days of 11:3 and 12:6 and to the "time, times and half a time" (three and a half years) of 12:14. The background for this time period seems to be the three and a half years during which the Jews suffered under the Syrian tyrant Antiochus Epiphanes (167-164 B.C.). It had become symbolic for a limited period of unrestrained evil.

**3-6**

We now meet the two witnesses. Like the four horsemen of chapter 6 and the 144,000 of chapter 5, the identity of these two witnesses has long intrigued New Testament scholars. While we may not be able to identify them with absolute certainty, we are able to understand their mission and destiny.

The two witnesses are dressed in sackcloth (the garment of mourning and penitence; see Matt. 11:21). Anyone who would harm them is devoured by fire from their mouths. They can shut up the sky so it will not rain; they can turn water into blood and strike the earth with any sort of plague they wish. They exercise this authority during the time of their prophesying—1,260 days or 42 months (solar months have thirty days).

As I understand Revelation, the two witnesses represent the church in the last days before the end. They are modeled after Moses, who turned water to blood (Exod. 7:14-18) and smote the earth with every plague (Exod. 7—11), and Elijah, who consumed his enemies with fire (2 Kings 1:10-12) and kept the heavens from raining (1 Kings 17:1). It was a common Jewish expectation that these two would return before the end of the age (Mal. 4:5; John 6:14; Deut. 18:15).

Like these two great leaders of Israel, the New Testament church is to proclaim its message with boldness until the very end. God will see to it that nothing silences the witnessing church until its mission is accomplished.

The two witnesses are also identified as the two olive trees and the two lampstands that stand before the Lord.

The background is the vision in Zechariah 4. The two olive trees in this Old Testament vision are Joshua, the high priest, and Zerubbabel, the Jewish governor. The people of God combine these roles. They are a "royal" (Zerubbabel) "priesthood" (Joshua), called to "declare the praises of him who called [them] out of darkness into his wonderful light" (1 Pet. 2: 9).

**7-10**

When the two witnesses have completed their task, they are attacked and killed by the beast of the abyss. This is the first mention of the beast, the great persecutor of the church in the last days. We will learn a great deal about this figure in chapters 13 and 17. For the present, note that he comes up from the abyss, the place of demons (see Luke 8: 31; Rev. 9: 1-11). He is demonic in nature, a powerful ally of Satan. It must also be noted that it is not until the witnesses have completed their mission that the beast is allowed to prevail. Until the very end, God remains in control.

The bodies of the witnesses lie in the street of the great city for three- and a-half days, during which time the inhabitants of the earth celebrate the death of their tormentors. In eastern lands it was considered a great disgrace to be deprived of a proper burial. We see the church in the last days persecuted and scattered by the world. The world scornfully denies burial to the defeated minority, whose death is cause for great celebration.

The city in which the witnesses lie martyred is figuratively called Sodom and Egypt—that is, it is like each of these places in some way. Sodom symbolized moral degradation (Gen. 19: 4-11), and Egypt stands for oppression and slavery. Elsewhere in Revelation the "great city" consistently refers to Rome (16: 19; 17: 18; etc.). Because the clause "where also their Lord was crucified" is added, many commentators have taken the city to be Jerusalem.

John wrote Revelation in terms of his own historical setting. Rome was the great enemy of the church. Emperor worship threatened the young congregations scattered throughout the empire. Rome is the beast who would, by its absolute power, force its will on all believers.

But in a fuller sense, John writes of the actual consummation of world history that is still future. Rome is not simply an ancient and powerful city. It is also the concentration of brute force, which in the last days will launch an all-out attack upon God and his people.

The symbols of Revelation are taken from the first century but find their complete fulfillment only at the end of time. Thus "the great city" in verse 8 is not simply the Rome of John's day. It is rather the debased sexuality of Sodom and the cruel oppression of Egypt, which characterize the totalitarian regime that will control all mankind at the end. It is the eschatological Rome. Since it is the essence of all that is unrighteous, it can also be considered the place where our Lord was crucified.

## 11-12

After the three- and a-half days when the witnesses' dead bodies lie exposed, God brings them back to life, and they rise to their feet. One is reminded of Ezekiel's vision of the valley of dry bones, brought to life by the breath of God (Ezekiel 37). While the enemies of righteousness stand by struck dumb with terror, a loud voice summons the church to heaven. It rises in a cloud in full view of the astonished world. This is certainly the rapture of the church. It is no secret.

Although the rapture is pictured in chapter 11, it does not necessarily take place before the events in the next few chapters, which still picture believers on earth. The Book of Revelation is not written sequentially, but in the order in which John received the visions. Here he is given an indication of the church's future vindication.

In summary, the account of the two witnesses teaches that the church will carry out its fundamental mission of bearing witness until the very end. The vast majority of men will not repent and believe. When the church's mission is complete, it will appear that Satan has won a total victory over the people of God. But God will intervene and vindicate forever those who have placed their trust in him.

**13-14**

As the two witnesses are taken up in a cloud, the city is rocked by a violent earthquake. A tenth of the city collapses, and seven thousand persons are killed. In Jewish thought, earthquakes are associated with periods of divine visitation. When God came down upon Mount Sinai "the whole mountain trembled violently" (Exod. 19:18). Throughout Revelation earthquakes accompany critical moments of divine activity—in 6:12 when the sixth seal is broken, in 8:5 when fire from the heavenly altar is cast upon the earth, in 11:19 when the heavenly temple is opened, and in 16:17-18 when the final bowl is poured out.

The survivors of the earthquake are terrified and give glory to God. This does not mean that they will repent and become believers. It only means that they acknowledge his superior power and might as demonstrated by his control over nature. It does not imply personal trust or a redemptive relationship.

Verse 14 notes that the second woe is now passed and a third is coming soon.

**15-18**

When the seventh trumpet sounds, we would expect

the third woe (as in 9:1, 13); but instead, we hear loud voices from heaven proclaiming that all earthly domination has been transferred to God. It is the long-awaited declaration that God has triumphed over evil and established his eternal reign. While in one sense this act was accomplished on the cross, in another sense it awaits a future manifestation. It is that moment in time when every knee shall bow and every tongue confess (Phil. 2:10-11). The church lives in the interim period between the defeat of Satan and his final expulsion. To grasp the certainty of both events is to live victoriously in the present.

The twenty-four elders fall before God, adoring and thanking him for taking his power and entering into his reign. God is the Almighty. None can stand before his awesome power. He was and he is. No longer is he the one who is to come, because from a prophetic perspective he is already here. He has begun his eternal reign. The nations rose in wrath, and God has answered in holy anger. The time for final judgment has arrived. This judgment anticipated by the elders will be carried out at the great white throne of 20:11-15. Those who destroy the earth are to be destroyed. God tailors the punishment to fit the crime.

For the righteous, however, it will be a time of reward. The saints, that is, those who reverence the name of God, whether they be prominent or relatively unknown, will all share in the reward of their faithful commitment to Christ.

**19**

In response to the elders' hymn of thanksgiving (vv. 17-18), the temple in heaven is opened, revealing the ark of the covenant. In the Old Testament, the ark was a sacred chest that symbolized the presence of God with his people. In John's vision, the ark would be a reminder of God's faithfulness in keeping his covenant promises during the difficult days that lay ahead. The lightning, thunder, earthquake, and hail correspond to the wrath God is about to pour out upon an unrepentant world.

## QUESTIONS

1. What does it mean to measure the temple?
2. What does the outer court stand for?
3. Who are the Gentiles who trample the outer court?
4. What is the source for the forty-two months? What do they stand for?
5. After which two Old Testament characters are the two witnesses modeled? How do you know this?
6. Who do the two witnesses stand for?
7. Explain the reference to Zechariah's vision of the two olive trees. What does it say about the two witnesses?
8. Who is the beast?
9. What is the significance that the beast comes up from the abyss?
10. As interpreted in light of the last days, what does the "great city" stand for? Why can it be called Sodom and Egypt?
11. Can modern America justly be called Sodom? Explain. Is America also Egypt? In what ways?
12. Why will men rejoice when the witnessing church is silenced?
13. What detail in the chapter illustrates the contempt that evil men have for believers?
14. What does it mean that the two witnesses are raised to life?
15. Why will the rapture of the church not be secret?
16. What is the response of those who survive the

earthquake in verses 13 and 14?

17. What does it mean that the kingdom of this world becomes the Kingdom of God?

18. On what basis do the twenty-four elders praise God?

19. What is the lot of believers in the coming judgment?

# REVELATION
# TWELVE

THE SEALS, TRUMPETS, and bowls are the three series of plagues in the Book of Revelation. As the seven seals are loosed, the scroll of destiny is opened to reveal the approach of the end. The seven trumpet plagues announce the end, and call men to repentance. Now, just before the bowls of God's wrath are poured out (chapters 15—16), John is taken behind the scenes of history to learn the basic reason for the hostility about to break upon the church. To realize that the coming persecution is the death struggle of an already defeated foe will encourage believers to hold fast until the ordeal is over.

**1-6**

John's vision opens with the appearance in the sky of

a woman who is clothed with the sun. The moon is under her feet, and a crown of twelve stars adorns her head. The scene portrays both authority and splendor. The woman is about to give birth to a child.

A second sign appears—a great red dragon with seven heads and ten horns. Upon his heads are royal crowns (the woman's crown is a *stephanos,* victory wreath, while the dragon's crowns are *diademata,* royal crowns). His horns symbolize the dragon's power. With his enormous tail, he sweeps stars from the sky and hurls them down to earth. The dragon positions himself in front of the woman, in order to devour the child the moment it is born.

These figures are not difficult to identify. The woman is not Mary the mother of Jesus, but the true Israel through whom Jesus, in terms of his human nature, entered into history (see Rom. 1:3). This interpretation is consistent with the fact that later in the same chapter the woman becomes the church, the "Israel of God" (Gal. 6:16). In the Old Testament, the enemies of Israel are often portrayed as dragons (Ps. 74:14; Isa. 27:1, KJV). John's readers would immediately recognize the great red dragon as Satan, the archenemy of God and his people, and he is specifically identified in verse 9.

The child to be born is Christ. He is the male child destined to rule the world with a rod of iron. The dragon's eagerness to devour the child explains the violent antagonism Jesus met during his earthly ministry. It began with the slaughter of the male children in Bethlehem (Matt. 2:16) and ended on a cross outside the city of Jerusalem.

But Satan's plans are thwarted. The child is snatched up to God and his throne (a reference to the ascension). When he returns, he will rule the nations with an iron scepter (19:15). This figure does not refer to a period during which Christ will govern the world with great severity. As the shepherd used his staff to protect his flock from marauding beasts, so will Christ strike down the enemies of righteousness who oppress and persecute his church. The rod of iron is judgment not governance.

When the child is taken up to heaven, the woman flees to a desert sanctuary prepared by God. There she remains for 1,260 days, protected and nourished by God for a period of time that corresponds with her time of persecution (see 11:2; 13:5). The church needs to know that in the troubled days ahead God will provide a spiritual refuge for believers so they can withstand the violent opposition of Satan.

**7-9**

John now records a war that takes place in heaven. The combatants are Michael and his angels, pitted against the dragon and his angels. The forces of righteousness prevail, and the dragon and his defeated army are hurled to the earth. This does not depict the primordial expulsion of Satan, the fallen angel. The scene is eschatological. It enters the narrative to explain the intense hostility the church will experience in the last days. When the devil is cast out of heaven, he "is filled with fury, because he knows that his time is short" (v. 12).

The church must recognize that there is a basic antipathy between God and Satan, right and wrong, believer and unbeliever. James put it unequivocally, "friendship with the world is hatred toward God" (James 4:4). Jesus said, "If they persecuted me, they will persecute you also" (John 15:20). Satan, who failed in his assault upon heaven, goes off in the last days to make war against the offspring of the woman—"those who obey God's commandments and hold to the testimony of

Jesus" (v. 17). Behind the scenes of history lie the eternal purpose of God and the oppositions of Satan. This insight reveals the root cause of the believer's difficulties and should encourage his endurance under trial.

The dragon is identified in three ways:

(1) He is that ancient serpent who leads the whole world astray. The obvious reference is to the historic encounter between Eve and the serpent in the garden of Eden (Gen. 3). Deceit has always been the *modus operandi* of Satan. Should he ever tell the truth, his evil intentions would be laid bare.

(2) The dragon is Satan. Originally the word *Satan* was not a proper name. It simply meant adversary. In time it came to stand for *the* adversary, Satan. He is the prosecutor who accuses men in the court of heaven (Job 1: 6-12).

(3) The dragon is also called the devil, which means slanderer. By means of accusation and slander, he tries to lead the whole world astray. Having fallen from heaven, he now desires to take as many as possible with him into the torments of hell (20:10, 15).

**10-12**

Revelation contains a number of passages best described as dramatic outbursts of praise. Verses 10-12 furnish one of the finest examples (also such passages as 4: 8; 7: 10; 19:1-2). A loud voice proclaims that the sovereign rule of God has become a reality. With it come authority and deliverance. Christ shares in this reign.

The great accuser has been hurled from heaven. He no longer enjoys the privilege of a heavenly courtroom in which to level accusations night and day against the brethren (compare Rom. 8: 33-34). He was overcome not only by the death of the Lamb but by the faithful testimony of the believing church as well. Satan is now a defeated foe! Expelled from heaven and rendered powerless by the cross, he is helpless against those who are willing to forfeit their lives in faithful obedience.

The defeat of Satan causes great rejoicing in heaven. At the same time, it brings woe to earth, because the devil has come down, full of fury, knowing his time is about up. This explains the suffering of the righteous during the last climactic period of history.

**13-17**

Following the hymn of praise which interrupted the narrative of Satan's expulsion from heaven, John continues the account. The dragon, recognizing his defeat by the hosts of heaven, now directs his hostility toward the woman who gave birth to the male child. The woman is the ideal Israel. Now that Christ has ascended to the throne of God, the woman is the New Testament church. This shifting of symbols is common in apocalyptic literature (earlier the woman was the righteous remnant within Judaism). A good example is Revelation 17:9, where the seven heads are seven hills and also seven kings.

Satan pursues the woman, but she is given the wings of an eagle and flies off to a place prepared for her in the desert. In Old Testament thought, the desert is often held to be a place of divine protection and nurture. For forty years God provided for his people in the wilderness. Hosea told of God luring Israel into the desert in order to speak tenderly to her (Hos. 2:14). The woman is to be kept in the desert out of the serpent's reach for the period of final turmoil, designated "a time, times and half a time" (forty-two months or three- and one-half years). Her protection is spiritual.

In his zeal to get at the woman, the serpent spews out a great river of water. He would sweep her away, but the earth opens its mouth and swallows the torrent. The scene depicts the intensity of satanic hatred against the church. Although we are obviously dealing with metaphors (the earth has no "mouth"), the truths they communicate are as real as if they had been phrased in nonmetaphorical language.

The dragon, enraged at this turn of events, goes away to make war against the rest of the woman's offspring, instead of the male child, Jesus. Verse 17 defines the rest of the offspring as "those who keep God's command-ments and hold to the testimony of Jesus." The fluid nature of apocalyptic language makes it possible for the church to be symbolized both by the woman and by her offspring.

The major point of this chapter is that because Satan has been defeated in heavenly battle, he is now going to take out his anger upon God's children on earth.

## QUESTIONS

1. Who is the radiant woman of verse 1?
2. From your knowledge of how the number *seven* is used in Revelation, what is the significance of the dragon's seven heads and seven crowns?
3. Who is the male child to be born?
4. What does it mean to rule with a rod of iron?
5. What event in the life of Christ is symbolized by the child being snatched up to heaven?
6. What does the desert stand for in Jewish literature? What would it suggest in modern literature? What does this imply about the necessity of a proper understanding of biblical backgrounds for proper interpretation?
7. What does the word *Satan* mean? In what way is Satan a "satan" today?
8. What does the word *devil* mean? Is it possible for

Christians to be "devils"?

9. On what basis is the believer today able to overcome the devil (see 12:11)?

10. What accounts for the devil's fury during the final period of history?

11. How is God's protection of the church in the last days described?

12. Why is this protection to be interpreted as spiritual rather than physical?

13. Do you have a "desert" in which Satan cannot reach you? Where is it?

14. Who are the rest of the woman's offspring?

# REVELATION
# THIRTEEN

THE FIRST SENTENCE of chapter 13 belongs to the preceding chapter (designated 12:18 in the Greek text). It is the dragon (not John as the King James Version has it) who stands on the shore of the sea. From that vantage point, he can call forth the first of two great beasts who are to carry out his campaign against the woman's offspring.

**1-4**

John sees a beast emerging from the sea. Like his master, the great red dragon, the beast has ten horns and seven heads (compare 12:3). In Revelation the number seven stands for completeness. A seven-headed beast would signify the ultimate enemy of the church. The blasphemous names inscribed on the seven heads reflect the growing tendency within the Roman Empire to consider the emperor as a divine being. Domitian (who was emperor at the time John had his visions) wanted to be addressed as "Our Lord and God."

The beast combines characteristics of the leopard, bear, and lion. It is helpful to note that the prophet Daniel used the same three animals (plus a fourth) to represent four historic kingdoms hostile to the people of God (Dan. 7: 3-8, 17, 23). Against this background, John is saying that the beast out of the sea epitomizes all worldly opposition to the Kingdom of God. Of crucial importance is the fact that the power and authority exercised by the beast have been given to him by Satan.

And who is this beast? In John's vision the beast is the Roman Empire. It is that concentration of secular power that claims a religious sanction for its cruelty and injustice. Yet the beast is more than the Roman Empire. It is that spirit of godless totalitarianism that has energized every authoritarian system of man throughout history. At the end of time, it will appear in its most malicious form. It will be the ultimate expression of deified secular authority.

John notes that one of the beast's seven heads had received what appears to have been a fatal wound. The wound, however, had been healed. In chapter 17 we will receive an interpreting angel's explanation of the beast and his seven heads (17: 8-17). For the moment it is enough to note that the beast possesses remarkable powers of recuperation. He appeared to have been dealt a fatal blow but has recovered.

Secular power has often been dealt a fatal blow in its long history of oppression but has always survived. The eschatological beast will bear the mark of this agelong struggle. The whole world is astonished at the recuperative power of the beast. Men worship the dragon (Satan) because he gives his authority to the state. Men worship the state because nothing can match its awesome power or wage a successful war against it. The Roman Empire supplied John with the outline of a cruel and despotic foe. The world has yet to see how terrifying this beast will be in its final incarnation.

**5-8**

The beast was given a mouth (that is, caused to speak) to utter proud words, even blasphemies. Four times in the Greek text of verses 5-7 we read the passive "was given." This emphasizes the subordinate role of the beast. He operates at the bidding of his master Satan. The time of his delegated authority is forty-two months (a span of time well understood by now, see 11:2-3; 12:6, 14). Throughout this section there are a number of phrases that echo the prophet Daniel (for instance, the little horn of Dan. 7:8 with its "mouth that spoke boastfully").

The beast is a blasphemer. He slanders the name of God (that is, the character of God as revealed in his name), his dwelling place, and those who live in heaven. In 2 Thessalonians 2:4 we have a somewhat parallel passage in which the "man of lawlessness" (the Antichrist) "exalts himself over everything that is called God . . . proclaiming himself to be God."

In John's day, the blasphemy of the beast was the increasing tendency to deify the Roman state by granting divine titles to its emperors and erecting temples in which to worship the spirit of Rome. In the last days, the secular state will wield extraordinary power and attempt to validate its role by religious sanctions.

Evil disguised as good is the ultimate lie. From recent history we have learned that an entire civilized nation can be led into accepting blatant error as long as the lie is big enough and told often enough. Christians need to stay alert to all the devious and seductive ploys of Satan.

The beast wars against the saints and conquers them. Although overcome physically, the church is yet the victor. In Revelation 15:2 we will read of those in heaven who were "victorious over the beast." True victory for the believer is to remain faithful in the crucial test of faith. The authority given to the beast extends to all men everywhere. All the inhabitants of the earth (genuine believers excluded) will worship the beast.

During his earthly ministry Jesus warned of false Christs who will "deceive even the elect—if that were possible" (Matt. 24:24). He himself was tempted to worship secular power (Matt. 4:8-10)—a temptation that in the final days will capture the allegiance of all whose names are not recorded in the Lamb's book of life.

The idea of a divine register is common in biblical thought. It is the Lamb's book, for eternal life is only possible because he was "slain from the creation of the world." The cross was no afterthought, necessitated by the Jew's rejection of an earthly kingdom. It belongs to the eternal decrees of God. Those who will be faithful in the coming trial have their names in that book of life.

**9-10**
At this point in the narrative a proverbial saying is introduced to teach that in the coming trial the believer must accept what God has ordained and not counter the state's brutality with force. The saying is composed of two short stanzas, each of which sets up a condition and gives the result. If the believer goes into captivity, then into captivity he will go. It is so ordained. If the believer takes up the sword to defend himself (the NIV is different here, in that it follows a different Greek textual tradition, which casts the verb into the passive voice), then he will be killed by the sword. John adds that this

prospect "calls for patient endurance and faithfulness on the part of the saints."

**11-17**

We come now to the second beast. As the first beast came out of the sea (from across the sea, from Rome to be specific), this beast comes "out of the earth" (from within Asia Minor itself). Elsewhere in Revelation the second beast is named the false prophet (16:13; 19:20; 20:10). He is a deceiver. His "two horns like a lamb" suggest gentle persuasion.

In view of his role as a miracle worker, who deceives the inhabitants of the earth, it is best to understand his speaking "like a dragon" as a reference to the beguiling speech of the serpent in the garden of Eden. As the first beast exercised the authority of the dragon, the second beast exercises the authority of his immediate superior. The evil trinity is now complete—Satan, the beast, and the false prophet.

Who is the false prophet? In John's vision, the beast was Rome with its claim to absolute power. The false prophet would be the local priests in Asia Minor who enforced the imperial cult of emperor worship. In relation to the last days, the false prophet symbolizes spurious religious authority bent on making man worship secular power. Certain religious groups even today seem totally committed to the destruction of basic New Testament Christianity.

The role of the false prophet is to make men worship the beast whose fatal wound was healed. In spite of numerous defeats, secular humanism revises and lays claims to man's devotion. In carrying out his task, the false prophet is enabled to perform miracles. Like a new Elijah preparing the way for a new "messiah," he causes fire to come down from heaven (1 Kings 18:38). Whether or not these are real miracles makes no particular difference for our interpretation (see 2 Thess. 2: 9). They accomplish their goal of leading men astray.

The false prophet orders the people to erect an image of the beast. He then gives breath to the image, causing it to speak. All those who refuse to worship the image are to be put to death. This demand will bring about a clear division between those who are willing to pay the price of their faith and those who would rather capitulate to the satanic religion of Antichrist. This defection is the great apostasy, which precedes the return of Christ. Nominal Christians do not forfeit their lives for a cause in which they really do not believe.

Economic boycott is another tactic of the false prophet. Everyone who would buy or sell must have the mark of the beast on his right hand or forehead. This mark is the numerical equivalent of the name of the beast. A favorite pastime in ancient days, when letters of the alphabet served as numbers, was to produce a riddle by giving a name in its numerical equivalent. To decipher the name from the number was a challenge.

One famous graffito from Pompeii reads, "I love her whose number is 545." The Jews called the practice *gematria*. The number of the beast, which was to be placed on the forehead or hand, was 666 (according to v. 18).

**18**

Verse 18 is the most enigmatic in the Book of Revelation. It challenges the reader to identify the beast by working backwards from the numerical equivalent of his name. No wonder the verse begins with the assertion, "This calls for wisdom."

The literature on Revelation is well stocked with proposed answers. Irenaeus (a second-century theologian who lived in Asia Minor) offers such suggestions as *Lateinos* (the Roman Empire) and *Teitan* (the Titans of

Greek mythology), but admits that the solution escapes him. A commonly held answer is Nero Caesar, but this has a number of difficulties as well.

Some writers take 666 in a symbolic sense to indicate a trinity of imperfection. One writer, taking his clue from Revelation 17:11 (in which the beast is said to be an eighth king), has discovered that all numbers up through 8 when added together equal 36, and that all the numbers up through 36 when added together equal 666. Thus 666 would not refer to any certain person; it would simply stand for the beast.

If John's intention was to camouflage the identity of the beast, we can only conclude that he was eminently successful. The riddle remains!

## QUESTIONS

1. What practice within the Roman Empire may account for the blasphemous names written on the seven heads of the beast?
2. What Old Testament passage may have suggested the leopard, bear, and lion?
3. What does the fatal wound that was healed suggest?
4. How can you account for the fact that men worship the dragon?
5. Describe the activity of the beast.
6. In John's day, who or what was the beast?
7. Who or what in the last days will be the beast?
8. In what way does the beast conquer the saints?
9. What does it mean to have your name written in the Lamb's book of life?
10. Explain the proverbial statement in verse 10.
11. Who was the second beast in John's vision?

12. In what role will the second beast appear in the last days?
13. What means did the false prophet use to cause men to honor the beast?
14. What could be some modern counterparts to these practices?
15. What is the mark of the beast?
16. Explain *gematria*.

# REVELATION
# FOURTEEN

AS YOU READ THROUGH Revelation you will notice that here and there among the darker scenes of judgment and persecution are bright glimpses of the blessedness awaiting the faithful. Chapter 13 was a somber reminder of what lies ahead. Suddenly we are lifted up out of the path of the approaching storm and placed with the faithful on Mount Zion. The obvious purpose of this vision is encouragement.

**1-5**

John once again sees the Lamb. In chapter 5 it was the Lamb who was worthy to open the scroll of destiny. In chapter 7 he received the worship and praise of the innumerable multitude who emerged from the great tribulation. Now he stands on Mount Zion—that sacred place long associated with divine deliverance—with the 144,000. These are the faithful who in chapter 7 were sealed against spiritual harm. In contrast to the inhabitants of the earth who are branded with the mark of the beast, the 144,000 have the name of the Lamb (and God's name) on their foreheads. They belong to the Lamb.

John hears a great sound from heaven, which he describes as the roar of a cataract and as the swelling crescendo of an ensemble of harpists. It is the 144,000 who lift their voices to sing "a new song"—the anthem of redemption, which no one can learn except those who have paid the price of endurance and experienced the joy of deliverance. Not even the angelic hosts can sing such a song.

The 144,000 are described in three ways:

(1) They are those who have not defiled themselves with women. Some commentators take this in a literal fashion, holding that it refers to an elite group of saints who have renounced all sexual relationships. Others interpret it as referring to those who have kept themselves from adultery and fornication. I prefer a more metaphorical interpretation. Israel in the Old Testament is often spoken of as a virgin (1 Kings 10:21; Jer. 18:13). Idolatry was portrayed as spiritual harlotry (Hos. 2). Correspondingly, the 144,000 are the bride of Christ who as they await his return have not defiled themselves by lusting after the pagan world system.

(2) They are those who are followers of the Lamb. They walk as he walked. In their daily lives, they carry out his instructions.

(3) They are a sacrificial offering to God. Having been purchased by the blood of the Lamb, they offer themselves to God for his purposes. In stark contrast with evil men who love and practice falsehood (22:15), the

144,000 are blameless—no lie is found in their mouths.
**6-7**

In rather quick sequence, we hear from three angels.
The first angel summons mankind to worship the
creator (vv. 6-7), the second announces the downfall of
Babylon (Rome) and the great harlot (v. 8), and the third
portrays the torment coming upon those who bear the
mark of the beast (vv. 9-11).

The first angel flies in midair so that all can hear what
he is about to say. The eternal gospel he proclaims is not
the good news of God's redemptive activity in Jesus
Christ, but as the following verse indicates, it is a call for
men to fear and worship God the creator. The message is
for all men everywhere. The hour of judgment has come.
To fear God is to hold him in reverence; to give him
glory is to honor him for who he is and all he has done.

This final call to worship is based upon God's action
in creation. In Romans 1:18-20, Paul established that
men are without excuse, because God has revealed himself in creation. It is on the same basis that the angel now
makes one last appeal.

**8**

A second angel follows the first and proclaims the fall
of Babylon the Great. The ancient city of Babylon in
Mesopotamia was the political and religious capital of a
world empire. It was known for its affluence and moral
corruption. In John's day, Rome was a contemporary
Babylon, symbolizing the spirit of godlessness that
draws men away from the worship of God.

Babylon is described as having made the nations
drink the maddening wine of her adulteries. The picture
that emerges is of a prostitute seducing the world by the
intoxicating influence of her corrupt practices. This
theme is developed fully in chapter 18. Babylon has
fallen in the sense that God has decreed that it be so. The

decree allows it to be prophetically declared as *fait accompli*. It is interesting that the announcement takes on the wording of the prophet Isaiah in his oracle against ancient Babylon (Isa. 21:9).

**9-11**

A third angel now proclaims the fate of those who choose to worship the beast and bear his mark. They will drink the wine of God's fury and be tormented forever with burning sulfur. The first figure draws upon the Old Testament practice of picturing the wrath of God as a draft of wine (Job 21:20; Ps. 75:8). The wine of God's fury has been poured full strength into the cup of his wrath.

The Bible does not support the notion that divine wrath is nothing more than the consequence of breaking some impersonal laws of nature (for example, obesity is the penalty for overeating). The wrath of God is his righteous response to man's refusal to accept his love. Since sin is personal, so is God's response to sin.

The second figure, torment with burning sulfur (the Greek says fire and sulfur, or brimstone) reflects God's judgment upon the ancient cities of Sodom and Gomorrah (Gen. 19:24). It is perhaps the most vivid symbol in the New Testament. To suffer forever in a sea of burning sulfur staggers the mind. Many modern writers object to the doctrine of eternal punishment on the basis that it is impossible to reconcile it with Jesus' teaching on love. Yet it was this same Jesus who taught that it would be better to cut off a hand and go through life maimed than live with two hands and go into hell "where the fire never goes out" (Mark 9:44).

Even if the fire of hell should prove to be no more than an apocalyptic symbol, it still speaks of a terrifying experience of torment and eternal loss. We dare not discard the clear teaching of Scripture on hell, because we cannot grasp it fully or because it runs counter to our sensitivities. We should remember that as fallen human beings we have to a great extent lost our awareness of the seriousness of sin.

Those who worshiped the beast (both the pagan world and apostate believers—the latter group is implied in v. 12) are tormented in the presence of the Lamb and his holy angels. Believers had suffered public abuse before their antagonists; now the tables have been turned, and their oppressors suffer before a heavenly tribunal. There is no rest day or night. The smoke of their torment ascends forever.

**12**

The prospect of eternal torment calls for patient endurance on the part of the saints. Those who are tempted to relinquish their faith in Christ and agree to join in emperor worship should recognize that such a compromise has fatal and far-reaching consequences. Better to endure the momentary opposition than to yield and find oneself forever cut off from God. Saints are simply those who keep God's commandments and remain faithful to Jesus. The great apostasy referred to in 2 Thessalonians 2:3 testifies to the fact that in the final showdown many will be unwilling to pay the price of allegiance to Christ, which will involve physical suffering.

**13**

John hears a voice from heaven declaring the blessedness of those who die in the Lord. Faithfulness may lead to martyrdom, but those who forfeit their lives will be blessed because they will enter victoriously into an eternal rest. This is contrasted to the fate of apostate Christians and those who have never made any pretension of believing. Death for them means eternal fire.

The rest from labor that awaits the faithful has nothing to do with normal toil. It is the end of all the trials brought upon believers by the demands of emperor worship. The deeds that follow them are acts of resistance to the religious demands of the state. Wherever secular power has camouflaged its unlawful intentions by donning the respectable robes of religion, the result has been flagrant disregard for human rights. At the end of time, the world will witness this unholy alliance in its most monstrous configuration.

**14-16**

Chapter 14 closes with two visions of divine judgment. The first (vv. 14-16) pictures judgment as a grain harvest. John sees a reaper "like a son of man" seated on a cloud with a golden crown on his head and holding a sharp sickle in his hand. The reaper is Christ. He awaits the command from the heavenly temple to exercise judgment. The return of the warrior Messiah in chapter 19 will be another presentation of the same great event.

An angel comes out of the temple to tell the reaper to proceed with judgment, because the appointed time has come and the earth is ripe for harvest. The one seated on the cloud swings his sickle, and the earth is harvested. Some writers prefer to interpret verses 14-16 as the gathering of the righteous, but it is more consistent with the chapter as a whole to take the unit as a general portrayal of coming judgment. It is the separation of the wheat and tares.

**17-20**

The second vision of judgment is pictured as a vintage (the gathering of grapes to be pressed for wine). An angel with a sharp sickle steps forth from the temple. A second angel orders him to swing his sickle on the earth and gather the ripe grapes. This second angel comes from the heavenly altar and is in charge of the fire. In 8: 3-5, an angel at the golden altar offered incense to God along with the prayers of the saints. If this is the same angel, we may infer that the prayers of the faithful play a definite role in the judgment of the wicked.

The grapes are cut and thrown into the great wine-press of God's wrath. Any view of God that omits his wrath is defective. Without wrath against sin, the love of God would be no more than maudlin sentimentality. The holiness of God demands his wrath against unrighteousness. While God forgives sin, his righteous character forbids any final acceptance of those who reject his forgiveness.

In ancient days the grape harvest was trampled by foot in a trough. A duct took the juice to a lower basin. To trample grapes was messy business. In the Old Testament the grape harvest served as a common figure for the wrath of God on his enemies (Isa. 63:3; Joel 3:13).

In the Revelation passage, the grapes are trampled outside the city. As Jesus suffered "outside the city gate" (Heb. 13:12), so also will his righteous judgment take place there. As the wine flowed red from the press, so will the blood of the wicked flow from God's great winepress. The quantity of blood is staggering. It rises as high as the horses' bridles and sweeps out in a gigantic wave for almost two hundred miles. One person calculated the exact volume of blood and decided that not enough people have lived on earth to supply the demand. Obviously such a computation overlooks the hyperbolic nature of the statement. What it means is that the victory of Christ's return and the ensuing judgment will be absolutely unprecedented.

## QUESTIONS

1.  Why does John introduce a vision of heavenly praise at this point?

111

2. What does it mean to have the name of the Lamb written on one's forehead?
3. Who are the 144,000?
4. Why can't angels join in with the 144,000 as they sing the new song before the throne?
5. In what sense are the 144,000 virgins?
6. What does it mean to be purchased from among men?
7. What was the eternal gospel proclaimed by the angel who flew in midair?
8. On what basis should the inhabitants of the earth fear God and give him glory?
9. Why was Rome called Babylon? What will the final Babylon be like?
10. Why is Rome portrayed as a harlot?
11. What is the destiny of those who worship the beast?
12. What do verses 10-11 teach about hell?
13. Contrast the death of believers with that of unbelievers.
14. Who is the reaper on the white cloud? What does this final "grain harvest" depict?
15. What aspect of judgment is emphasized in the vision of the vintage?
16. If the flow of blood in verse 20 is not literal, what does it symbolize? Is it any less real?

# REVELATION
# FIFTEEN

IN CHAPTER 12 TWO SIGNS appeared in heaven—the radiant woman and the enormous red dragon. Now a third sign appears—seven angels with the seven last plagues. They are the *last* plagues, in that they bring to a close God's warning to impenitent man. They do not exhaust the wrath of God. The lake of fire remains for those whose names are not in the Lamb's book of life (Rev. 20:15).

**1-4**

We are about to enter into a third series of numbered plagues. Later in the chapter, the seven angels will be given golden bowls filled with the wrath of God (v. 7). In the following chapter, all seven bowls will be poured out upon the earth and its inhabitants. From a literary standpoint, the seven bowls are an unfolding of the seventh trumpet in the same way that the seven trumpets expanded the seventh seal.

The vision of the seven angels is interrupted by yet another vision (vv. 2-4). John sees what appears to be a sea of glass mixed with fire. Beside the sea stand those who have emerged victorious over the beast and his image. This means they have remained faithful to God in spite of all the threats and belligerent activity of the Antichrist and his henchmen.

The victors are presented harps, and they sing what John calls "the song of Moses . . . and the song of the Lamb." Exodus 15:1-18 records the song of Moses, which celebrates the Lord's historic deliverance of his people from Egyptian bondage. This deliverance prefigured a greater deliverance that would be achieved by the Lamb. It is on the basis of this great redemptive triumph that the overcomers of Revelation lift their voices to praise God for who he is and all he has accomplished.

The hymn itself may have been used in the early church. Practically every phrase reflects the rich vocabulary of the Old Testament (for instance, Ps. 111:2; Deut. 32:4; Mal. 1:11). With its focus on the greatness of God, it should serve as a model for modern hymnody.

God is the Almighty. He is able to carry through everything he has purposed to do. He is king of the ages, and his sovereignty knows no end. All nations will come to him in worship, because he alone is holy and his righteous acts have been made known to man. This act of universal recognition does not imply the personal salvation of all men. It is a way of stressing the comprehensiveness of God's righteous activity on behalf of man.
**5-8**
Following the victors' song of praise, John sees that the temple in heaven is opened. The sacred shrine is

more closely defined as the tabernacle (or tent) of testimony, which was the portable sanctuary in which God dwelt during Israel's wandering in the wilderness. It is called the tent of *testimony*, because it contained the two tablets of testimony Moses brought down from Mount Sinai (Deut. 10:5). In the present context, the opening of the tent suggests that the seven last plagues are to come from the presence of God, in fulfillment of his covenant relationship with those who have remained faithful.

From the temple emerge the seven angels of destruction. They are dressed in clean linen and have golden sashes around their chests. The role they are about to play is both priestly and royal. One of the four living creatures (those guardians of the throne in 4:6; 7:11; and 14:3) hands the angels bowls filled with the wrath of God. The reign of wickedness is almost over. God will vindicate himself before man. His wrath is about to be poured out upon all who have refused his love.

As the angels of destruction receive their bowls of wrath, the temple is filled with smoke (symbolizing the glory and power of God). God's presence is often accompanied by smoke (Exod. 19:18; Isa. 6:4). In John's vision the smoke serves to warn people that no one is allowed to enter the holy place until the seven last plagues have been poured out. No one can approach God until his wrath is complete. The time for repentance is over. The patience and long-suffering of God is exhausted. In the decrees of eternity the doors of access are closed and judgment has begun.


## QUESTIONS

1. Why are the bowl plagues called the last?

2. Who are those who stand beside the sea of glass?
3. Why can the song in verses 2-4 be called both the song of Moses and the song of the Lamb?
4. Why was it especially appropriate in John's day to be reminded that God was the Almighty?
5. What does it mean that God is king of the ages?
6. In what sense will the nations come and worship before God?
7. Why is the tabernacle of testimony brought up at this time? Where did it get its name?
8. What may be symbolized by linen and gold?
9. What is symbolized by the smoke in the temple?
10. Why is no one allowed in the temple until the bowls are poured out?

# REVELATION
# SIXTEEN

EVERYTHING IS NOW in readiness for the final series of
plagues. The seven angels of destruction have received
their bowls of divine wrath and await the command to
pour them out upon those who have chosen to follow
the beast.

There are a number of parallels between the trumpet
series and the bowl series. For example, in each series
judgment falls on the earth, sea, inland waters, and
heavenly bodies respectively. This has led some to view
the two series as covering the same events from two
different perspectives. But this runs counter to the
rather carefully worked out literary structure of the
book, in which each series is the expansion of the last

element of the previous series. It also overlooks the many distinctions between the series.

**1-3**

A loud voice from the temple (perhaps the voice of God since the temple is now closed to anyone else, 15:8) orders the seven angels to go and pour out the bowls of God's wrath. The first angel carries out his charge, and ugly, painful sores break out on everyone who bears the marks of the beast and worships his image.

The bowl judgments have a number of similarities to the ten Egyptian plagues (Exod. 7:14—12:30). For example, the ugly sores of the first bowl are like the boils and abscesses of the sixth Egyptian plague (Exod. 9:9-11). The sea of blood of the second bowl parallels the turning of the Nile into blood (Exod. 7:20-21). While the plagues of Revelation are not slavish copies of earlier disasters, they do employ the vocabulary traditionally used for such events.

Note that God's wrath falls on those who have declared themselves his enemies. God's people are nowhere to be found in this saga of divine judgment. While Christian believers may suffer at the hands of wicked men (not even Jesus, the perfect man, was immune from this), they will never experience the wrath of God poured out in the last days on the followers of the beast.

The second angel pours out his bowl on the sea. (The translation "bowl" is to be preferred to the King James Version's "vial," because the Greek word describes a shallow dish rather than a bottle. The contents of a bowl are quickly and easily poured out!)

The second bowl plague turns the sea into blood like that of a dead man—that is, coagulated and putrid. Everything in the sea dies. Recall that the second trumpet plague turned a third of the sea into blood, and that a third of the living creatures in the sea died (8:8-9). The limited consequence of the warning trumpets now gives way to the complete devastation of the bowl plagues.

**4-7**

The third bowl is poured out on the rivers and springs of water. They, too, become blood. Water is absolutely essential for life. God's judgment deprives the wicked of something they cannot live without. Death is the final reward for sin.

At this point the angel of the waters declares that God is just in his judgments. Followers of the beast have shed the blood of the righteous; it is, therefore, entirely appropriate that they should have to drink blood. The punishment fits the crime.

The angel "in charge of the waters" should probably be thought of as a supernatural being in some way connected with the rivers and springs that have just been turned to blood. God is described as the one who is and who was. Earlier in Revelation (1:4, 8; 4:8), he was also the one who is to come. This can now be omitted, because the final sequence of events is already under way. God has come in judgment.

The altar adds its testimony to the angel's declaring that the judgments of God are true and just. They are fully deserved and carried out with fairness. God is addressed both as Lord (absolute sovereign) and Almighty (nothing lies beyond his power to achieve). He is the ultimate judge of all men, and none can stay his hand.

**8-9**

The fourth angel pours out his bowl of divine wrath upon the sun. When the fourth trumpet blew, a partial eclipse followed (8:12), but the fourth bowl gives power to the sun to scorch the inhabitants of the earth with an intense heat. (The Greek text reads, "And men were scorched with a great scorching.") It would seem that such intense pain would cause people to repent of their evil ways and acknowledge the supremacy and greatness of God. But this is not the case. Instead they curse the very name of God, even though they are fully aware that he is the one who has brought about the plagues. Their commitment to evil is so complete that repentance is no longer possible. To serve the beast is to become like the beast!

**10-11**

The fifth bowl is poured out on the throne of the beast, and his kingdom is plunged into darkness (compare the ninth Egyptian plague, Exod. 10:21-19). The darkness intensifies the people's distress, and they gnaw their tongues in agony. It is not a pretty picture. Justice demands that the intensity of divine retribution correspond to the seriousness of rejecting divine love. Men curse God for their pains and sores but refuse to repent. Earlier we read that the beast "opened his mouth to blaspheme God" (13:6). Now his followers, who have taken on the character of their master, curse (or blaspheme) the name of God. We inevitably become like the one to whom we give our allegiance.

**12-14**

The sixth angel of destruction pours out his bowl on the Euphrates River. Its waters dry up, in order to prepare a way for the kings of the East. The Euphrates marked the eastern boundary of the Roman Empire. The land beyond the river was controlled by the Parthians, an enemy nation greatly feared by the Romans. For the Euphrates to dry up would symbolize the imminent danger of invasion from without. The kingdom of the beast is about to be overrun (described in 17:15—18:24).

This destruction of ancient Rome foreshadows the

ultimate collapse of all secular power and authority at the end of history. There will be no gradual turning to truth until the entire earth is ready to accept the one they once spurned. On the contrary, God will break in suddenly to devastate the opposition and establish his sovereignty in human affairs.

John sees three unclean spirits like frogs come out of the mouths of the unholy trinity. This evil triumvirate consists of Satan, the beast, and the false prophet (the beast out of the earth in 13:11-17). The evil spirits are demonic and deceptive. The deceptive quality of evil men is stressed in the New Testament. Jesus warned that in the last days false prophets would lead men astray with signs and wonders (Matt. 24:24). Paul says that the coming of the lawless one will be with counterfeit miracles and deceit (2 Thess. 2:9-10). The specific role of the three demonic spirits in Revelation is to gather the kings of the entire world for battle on the day of God (described in 19:11-21). We will learn more of this battle site after a brief interruption.

**15**

As the end approaches believers are to remain alert. The risen Christ reminds the faithful of the unexpectedness of his return—"Behold, I come like a thief!" (compare Matt. 24:42-44; 1 Thess. 5:2). Blessed is the one who stays awake and keeps his clothes ready. He will not be caught naked at the return of Christ and be shamefully exposed. The point of the illustration is that the last days will require believers to be alert and discerning so the deceptive propaganda of Satan will not lead them astray.

**16**

The narrative resumes, and we learn that the three evil spirits gather the kings of the world to a place that bears the Hebrew name *Armageddon*. This cryptic reference has become one of the more widely discussed problems in Revelation. Where and what is Armageddon?

If you examine modern speech translations, you will discover that the word is often written Har Magedon. *Har* means "mountain," while *Ar* is probably "city." Megiddo is an important city that guards a strategic military road running between the coastal plain near Mount Carmel and the famous valley of Esdraelon. The valley is one of the most famous battlefields in history. Because there is no real mountain (*Har*) of Megiddo and because the city itself (*Ar*) doesn't seem a likely place for massive warfare, many writers have taken the designation as symbolic of the final overthrow of the forces of evil by God's power. It is a way of portraying the victory of righteousness over evil at the end of the age. It is described as warfare, in order to portray the conflict and victory in as vivid and meaningful terms as possible.

**17-21**

The seventh angel pours his bowl into the air, and a voice from the temple declares, "It is done!" The seven angels have completed their awesome task. Now follow lightning, thunder, and an earthquake more devastating than man has ever known. The great city (Rome) is split into three parts, and cities collapse around the entire world.

Writers differ about whether or not these physical phenomena should be taken in a literal sense. Will there be actual earthquakes, or is the earthquake a way of saying that every fortification raised by man against God will be utterly shattered in the coming judgment? The person who understands an earthquake in the physical sense must be careful not to miss the theological significance of the event. The person who takes the earthquake as a metaphor of divine intervention must guard against the tendency to consider it as poetry only. In both cases, something happens. God has given that great secular enemy of the church ("Babylon the Great"—symbol of luxury, cruelty, and vice) a cup filled with his passionate hatred of evil.

John's vision moves kaleidoscopically. The islands of the sea flee away. Mountains cannot be found. The sky opens and huge hailstones weighing up to a hundred pounds each crash down upon mankind. By this time it is no surprise that even this cataclysmic display is met by resistance on the part of men. Instead of repenting, they curse God for the plague of hail.

## QUESTIONS

1. What do the seven bowls contain?
2. What event in Old Testament history supplies a good deal of the imagery for the seven bowl plagues? How do you account for this?
3. Why is it fitting for the wicked to drink blood?
4. Why might the casual reader think that God's judgments were unjust? On what basis does Revelation argue that they are just?
5. Why doesn't scorching heat cause people to repent?
6. In John's day who would have been the kings from the East? What does their defeat symbolize?
7. Identify the unholy trinity.
8. List the tactics to be used by demonic spirits in the last days.
9. Who is speaking in the first part of verse 15?
10. Does verse 15 imply that the church is on earth until the very end?
11. Explain the difference between Armageddon and Har Magedon.

12. What does Armageddon stand for? Do you think it will be a literal battle fought with men and arms? Why or why not?
13. How would you go about explaining the cataclysmic events connected with the seventh bowl plague?
14. What is man's response to the plague of hail?

# REVELATION
# SEVENTEEN

WE ARE ABOUT to encounter yet another enemy of God and his people. This time it is a great licentious whore who sits astride a scarlet beast. She is the royal courtesan of the kings of the earth. Drunk with the blood of believers, she holds in her hand a golden goblet filled with the filth of her obscene profession. In chapter 19 we shall meet a totally different female figure—the bride of Christ dressed in "fine linen, bright and clean" (19:8). The contrast is obvious.

**1-2**

One of the seven bowl angels invites John to witness the punishment of the notorious prostitute. As we read through chapter 17 we will find several important figures interpreted for us. The woman is said to be "the great city that rules over the kings of the earth" (v. 18). Furthermore, the waters are the people of the world (v. 15), and the scarlet beast is the first beast of chapter 13 whose seven heads are seven hills and seven kings (vv. 8-9) and whose ten horns are ten kings who war against the Lamb (vv. 12-14). While the interpretation aids in identifying the harlot and the waters, it clouds the issue in connection with the beast, as we shall see later.

The Old Testament often speaks of religious apostasy as whoredom. For example, Hosea taught that Israel would be put to public shame because she had played the harlot with Canaanitish religious practices (see also Isa. 1:21; Jer. 2:24). In Revelation the harlotry of Rome (the prostitute) is not religious but relates to the seductive methods used by that powerful city to gain control of the entire world. She has committed adultery with the kings of the earth; that is, she has enticed them into compromising relationships. The nations are intoxicated with the wine of her adulteries. The supposed benefits of such alliances have made them lightheaded and unable to grasp what is happening.

**3-6**

John is now carried away in the Spirit to a desert place. There he sees a woman sitting on a scarlet beast with seven heads and ten horns. The beast is covered with blasphemous names. Roman emperors by the time of Revelation had often accepted or claimed titles implying deity. From the Christian's point of view this practice amounted to the worst kind of heresy. God alone is to be acknowledged as divine. To call a secular authority "Lord" would be a denial of God's unique role as universal sovereign.

The woman is dressed in the luxurious garments of

ancient royalty. Since purple and scarlet dyes were expensive to extract, they were used primarily by the very rich. The harlot is said to be glittering with ornaments of gold, precious gems, and pearls. The picture is one of wanton luxury and extravagance. Her ostentatious display of wealth testifies to the success of her immoral trade. In her hand she holds a golden cup "filled with abominable things and the filth of her adulteries." Her cup promises carnal delight, but it is filled with the sewage of her sensual practices.

On the harlot's forehead is a mysterious inscription. (Note: the NIV regards *mystery* as part of the inscription.) She is "BABYLON THE GREAT, THE MOTHER OF PROSTITUTES AND OF THE ABOMINATIONS OF THE EARTH." These titles indicate that by John's day Rome, like her earlier counterpart ancient Babylon, had become the epitome of vice, luxury, and power. She had led all the nations of the earth into her vile trade. Her abominable practices were found everywhere. Not content with her own debauchery, she had infected the entire earth with her lust and disease.

From Roman history we learn of an empress by the name of Messalina who used to leave the palace by night and serve as a whore in the public brothel. Some writers think that she was the one John had in mind as he described the great harlot.

John sees that the woman is drunk. It is not wine, however, that has caused her condition. She is drunk with the blood of the saints, those who have sacrificed their lives in faithful witness to Jesus. John is astonished. The vulgarity of the scene is more than he can cope with. As an expression of the true nature of the Roman Empire, the whore is overpoweringly repulsive.
**7-8**

The angel responds to John's amazement by indicating that he will explain the mystery of the woman and the beast. Reversing the order, the angel interprets first the beast (vv. 8-14) and then the woman (v. 18).

Of the beast it is said that he "once was, now is not, and will come up out of the Abyss." This appears to be a deliberate contrast to the glorified Christ of chapter 1 who says, "I am the Living One; I was dead, and behold I am alive for ever and ever!" (1:18; see 2:8, also the description of God in 1:4, 8, and 4:8). Deception is a major ploy of Satan's henchmen (13:13-15). If the beast for John was Rome as the persecutor of faithful believers, then the verse would indicate that while the church had at an earlier time experienced his hostility, at the moment they were in a period of temporary relief (he *was* but is not *now*). However, he is to come again.

In A.D. 60 Nero was that beast. He instigated a persecution of the Christians in order to avert suspicion that he had set fire to Rome. Both Peter and Paul were victims of this cruel hoax. In John's day the church was on the verge of a renewed persecution under Domitian. The beast was about to rise from the abyss.

Whenever in the course of history secular power has overstepped its lawful bounds and tyrannized the innocent, it can be said that the beast has risen from the abyss. At the end of history, he will rise to launch a final assault against the people of God, but on that occasion he will confront the King of kings who will dispose of him forever in the fires of perdition (19:20).

John reports that those whose names are not written in the book of life will be astonished when they see the beast. His recuperative powers are incredible. Evil seems to return from every defeat with renewed vigor, surviving every death stroke (13:3) to war again.

**9-11**

From this point on, the angel's explanation of the

beast becomes harder to follow. In anticipation the angel warns, "This calls for a mind with wisdom." A similar statement (13:18) accompanied the designation of 666 as the number of the beast. Neither section is crystal clear!

The angel explains that the seven heads of the beast are seven hills on which the woman sits. The first-century reader would immediately recognize a reference to Rome, the city built upon seven hills. So far so good. But now the angel goes on to say that the seven heads are also seven kings. The symbolism of apocalyptic literature must never be approached as some sort of inflexible linguistic code. Symbols are fluid and have a way of conforming to the contours of the immediate context. The seven heads are seven hills *and* seven kings simultaneously.

The plot thickens. Five kings have fallen, one currently is, and the seventh—when he comes—will remain only for a short time. What does all of this mean?

Many writers see this as a sequence of Roman emperors, with John living during the reign of the sixth. If it is true that John writes during the reign of Domitian (A.D. 81-96), it is possible to make him number six only by beginning with Caligula (A.D. 37-41) rather than Augustus (30 B.C.—A.D. 14) and skipping the three who ruled in quick succession during the brief period between Nero (A.D. 54-68) and Vespasian (A.D. 69-79). This exegesis is as bad as the arithmetic brought in to support it. Equally unsatisfactory is the attempt to interpret the seven kings as seven kingdoms.

The most reasonable approach is to see the seven kings, symbolizing the power of Rome, as a historic whole. Seven is the number of completeness. To be living under the sixth king with the prospect that the seventh would rule only for a short time would be a way of saying that the end of secular abuse and persecution is at hand. Roman domination is drawing to a close. God will soon intervene to vindicate the faithful and bring judgment upon the persecutors.

Verse 11 is the heart of the riddle. The beast is described as an eighth king who belongs to the seven. He is not simply one of the seven. While in one sense he belongs to the seven (he rules on earth as a king), in another sense he is distinct. As an eighth he stands outside and above the historical sequence of secular powers that have governed the empire up through John's day. In short, the beast is not a human ruler through whom the power of evil expresses itself—he is that evil power itself. The beast is none other than Antichrist, that malign and evil being who throughout the history of the church has set himself in opposition to the people of God (1 John 2:18). But he is "going to his destruction." No matter how terrible the beast may appear and how intimidating his claims, this oppressor will receive his just reward in the eternal fires of retribution.

**12-14**

The ten horns of the scarlet beast are said to be ten kings who have not yet received their kingdoms. When they do receive power and authority (even though it will be for a brief period only—"one hour"), they will turn it over to the beast. These ten kings are symbolic of all secular power in the last days. They will join forces with the Antichrist to make war against the Lamb. This great confrontation will take place when Christ, the warrior Messiah, returns to establish his sovereignty over a rebellious world order (19:11-21).

The angel declares that the Lamb will overcome the vast coalition of earthly powers because he is Lord of lords and King of kings. No force on earth can withstand the greatness of his power. He rules over all. With him will be his followers—the called, the chosen, the faithful. As they have been true to him in times of severest testing, they will share with him in his triumph over wickedness. The beast is to go down in defeat before the Lamb. Those who by faith have weathered the storm of satanic opposition will stand with their leader in his moment of victory.

**15-18**

The angel ends his extended interpretation of the beast and reveals the identity of the harlot and the waters upon which she sits. The waters are "peoples, multitudes, nations and languages," in other words, the entire inhabited world. No nation has escaped an adulterous alliance with the harlot Rome.

But now a sudden political shift takes place. Whereas the ten kings had given their authority to the scarlet beast and joined in battle against the Lamb, they now turn in fierce hatred against the prostitute. The rebellion of the kings reflects the law of political history that every revolution carries within itself the seeds of its own destruction. The fierceness of their hatred for the one who has brought them to defeat is seen in their vicious acts of retaliation. They strip her naked, eat her flesh, and burn her remains with fire—a ghastly ordeal that reveals man's evil nature striking out in blind fury against the supposed cause of its own wickedness.

The angel adds that God has put it into the hearts of the kings to carry out his purpose. In the final analysis, even the destructive wrath of evil men is used by God to fulfill his word.

Almost as an afterthought, the angel says that the woman in the vision is the great city that rules over the earth. Rome is that wicked harlot who has seduced the political powers to meet their own destruction.

# WHAT ARE WE WAITING FOR?

## QUESTIONS

1. Why is Rome portrayed as a harlot?
2. What were the blasphemous names that covered the scarlet beast?
3. Why could Rome appropriately carry the title "Babylon"? To what extent do you think modern America can rightly be designated "Babylon"?
4. What activity for Rome is symbolized by the fact that the whore is drunk with blood?
5. Of the various forms of government in the world today, which one would most appropriately be symbolized by a drunken whore? Why?
6. The beast who was, is not, and will be is a contrast with what other person in Revelation?
7. What does it mean in the course of history for the beast to arise from the abyss?
8. What two things are represented by the seven heads of the beast?
9. List three different approaches to the problem of who or what is represented by the seven kings.
10. In what sense does the beast belong to the seven kings yet is an eighth?
11. Who is the beast in this context?
12. To what later event in Revelation does the war between the beast (and the ten kings) and the Lamb refer?
13. On what basis will the Lamb overcome the coalition of ten kings and the beast?
14. What law of political history is illustrated by the rebellion of the kings and beast against the harlot?
15. In what sense is God involved in the devastation of the notorious prostitute?
16. Who is the prostitute?

# REVELATION EIGHTEEN

CHAPTER 18 IS a prophetic portrayal of the destruction of Rome. About two-thirds of the verses in the NIV are printed in poetic form because the various speakers in the chapter are drawing heavily upon prophetic oracles and taunt songs from the Old Testament. The fall of Rome is described in the lyric prose of prophets who raised their voices against the enemies of God's covenant people, Israel.

Some have claimed that the tone of the chapter is too vindictive to be genuinely Christian. Such criticism, however, fails to understand the nature of prophetic realism. The chapter portrays the ultimate collapse of an evil and cruel anti-Christian world order. Its rhetoric is appropriate to its message and must not be interpreted apart from its prophetic context.

**1-3**

John sees an angel descending from heaven. The angel possesses great authority, equal to his task of announcing the overthrow of all secular power. Coming from the presence of God, he illuminates the earth with his splendor. We are reminded of Moses, who had to veil himself when he returned from God's presence, because the radiance of his face frightened the people (Exod. 34:29-35).

The angel declares with the mighty voice, "Fallen! Fallen is Babylon the Great!" The words echo Isaiah 21:9. This announcement is true whenever the forces of evil are put to rout. In the last days, "Babylon" will fall in an ultimate sense. The angel proclaims the event as already having taken place, because from a prophetic standpoint God's decree is certain. It is beyond any possibility of change.

Since Babylon has fallen, the victory has already been won. The forces of Antichrist may go through the motions of conflict, but the outcome has already been determined. God is sovereign, and history is under his control. His victory is a major theme of the Book of Revelation.

By portraying Babylon as a haunt for evil spirits and unclean birds, the author is saying that the once-powerful and indulgent capital of world civilization is doomed to absolute desolation. Babylon has fallen because she has seduced the nations of the world to follow her corrupt and immoral life-style.

**4-8**

Another voice from heaven is heard calling the people of God out of the wicked city. Oracles against ancient Babylon by Isaiah and Jeremiah provide much of the rhetoric (consult a cross-reference Bible for specific parallels). Believers are to separate themselves from the great city that symbolized arrogant power and wanton luxury. Why? So that they will not be seduced into sharing her sinful way of life and consequently receive her plagues. In times of persecution, the church has been tempted to compromise its stand and come to terms with evil. God's way is to avoid unholy alliances.

Babylon symbolizes not only the ancient capital on the Euphrates but also first-century Rome and the eschatological stronghold of secular power as well. Babylon stands for man in his defiant opposition to the ways of God. Throughout history, the city appears wherever brute force and intrigue have manipulated people for the benefit of the few.

The sins of Babylon have been piled up until they reach heaven itself. God remembers her many crimes, and Babylon is to be paid back in the currency of her wickedness. She is to receive double for what she has done. She had offered her cup of immorality to the nations (14:8). Now she must drink the wrath of God from the same cup. She gave herself glory and luxury; now she is to receive a like amount of torment and grief.

Babylon is a proud and arrogant city. She boasts that she sits as a queen, not a widow. She is beyond personal loss. Her men do not lie dead on the field of battle. She will never have to mourn. Not so, declares a voice from heaven. Plagues will suddenly overtake her. Without warning, death, mourning, and famine will be her lot. She is to be consumed by fire when the Lord God, the mighty one, comes in judgment. Nothing was quite so devastating in ancient times as a city on fire. Babylon is to be consumed by raging flames. In the coming judgment, all human opposition to God will be destroyed.
**9-10**

The next eleven verses consist of three separate dirges

chanted by the kings of the world who have shared the luxury of Rome (vv. 9-10), the merchants who have grown rich supplying her demands (vv. 11-17a), and by the maritime industry, which has delivered from abroad whatever she craved (vv. 17b-19). Read Ezekiel's lamentation over Tyre (Ezekiel 27) to see the resemblance.

The kings of the earth who shared in Rome's illicit practices stand amazed as they watch her burn. Not about to rush to the rescue of their mistress, they watch her torment from afar. Terrified, they bewail the sudden destruction of the once-powerful capital of the world. The use of fire to depict the eschatological collapse of the world order is common in New Testament thought (see 2 Pet. 3:12). Throughout Scripture, fire is a symbol of judgment.

**11-17a**

The dirge is next taken up by the merchants of the earth. Their sorrow is not for Rome but for the collapse of their own financial empire. With Rome in flames, no one remains to buy their expensive merchandise. The list of imports emphasizes the excessive luxury of the capital city. Ancient sources indicate that many of the Roman emperors had an insatiable appetite for self-gratification. Nero spent $100,000 for Egyptian roses for one banquet. It is reported that Vitellius spent $20 million (mostly on food) during his reign of less than one year. Small wonder that greedy merchants around the world bewail the destruction of Rome!

Like the kings of the earth, the merchants stand far off, terrified by the great city's torment and mourning her demise. Each group interprets the disaster in terms of its own special interests. For the merchants it seems tragic that great wealth should be destroyed in a short time.

**17b-19**

The third group to lament the destruction of Rome

consists of those connected with the maritime industry. When they see the smoke of her burning, they throw dust on their heads and mourn. Since Rome was the center of the shipping industry, all who made their fortunes on the sea established home port there. How tragic the destruction of such an influential city.

**20**

Verse 20 is a momentary interruption in the narrative of Rome's fall. The "saints and apostles and prophets," who are called upon to rejoice over her fall, are not the church on earth but the church glorified. In the opening phrase, it is heaven that is to rejoice. God has judged Rome for the way she has treated the church. In time every injustice will be punished. God would not be moral if he failed to requite evil men for their selfishness and cruelty.

**21-24**

In verses 11-19, we saw the effect of Rome's fall on outsiders who were profiting from her excessive luxury. In the following verses, we see the effect of her fall on those who lived and worked within the city.

But first an act of prophetic symbolism: a mighty angel picks up a boulder the size of a large millstone and hurls it into the sea, saying that the great city of Babylon will be thrown down with equal violence. Babylon, of course, is Rome. And Rome in turn is the eschatological city of secular opposition to God. Both will suddenly disappear like a millstone thrown into the sea. When God acts in reprisal against his enemies, he does so suddenly and devastatingly.

The completeness of Rome's destruction is seen in the recurring phrases, "Will never be heard/be found/shine in you again" (six times in vv. 21-23). Silence falls upon the city. The glad sounds of harp and trumpet, voice and flute, are never to be heard again. The sound of craftsmen plying their trade has stopped. The lights are off. Marriages have ceased. Judgment has fallen because Rome's deceitful merchants have led the nations of the world astray. Rome is condemned because of her corrupt leadership and her immoral practices.

A final reason for Rome's fall is her persecution of the church. Her streets are red with the blood of Christian martyrs. As the center of opposition to Christ and the church, she is guilty of all innocent blood.

## QUESTIONS

1. On what basis can the angel declare that Babylon (Rome) has fallen since in John's time Rome still stood?
2. What does it mean that the nations have "drunk the maddening wine of her adulteries"?
3. From a good, cross-reference Bible, list the actual words and phrases in verses 4-8 that seem to come from Isaiah and Jeremiah.
4. In what sense is the church called out of the corrupt world in which it lives?
5. What does Rome mean by saying that she is not a widow?
6. Why do the kings of the earth lament the destruction of Rome?
7. Why do merchants mourn Rome's fall?
8. Why is the fall of Rome a disaster for seamen?
9. Why is heaven to rejoice over Rome's fall?
10. What is intended by the symbolic action of hurling a great stone into the sea?
11. On what basis can the final collapse of world civilization be compared to the fall of Rome?
12. List three reasons to account for Rome's fall.

# REVELATION
# NINETEEN

FOR SOME TIME NOW, John's visions have been dark and foreboding. Chapter 16 brought us the seven bowls of God's wrath. Chapter 17 portrayed the punishment of the great prostitute. Chapter 18 was taken up with the destruction of Rome. Against this bleak background, we now hear what has been called the hallelujah chorus of 19:1-8.

The word *hallelujah* means "Praise the Lord." It is found only in this passage in the New Testament. In chapter 18 we heard three laments (by kings, merchants, and seamen). Now three separate groups (a heavenly multitude, twenty-four elders and four living creatures, and a voice from the throne) respond in praise to God.

**1-5**

The great multitude lifts its voice in praise because

God has condemned the harlot and taken revenge for the blood of his servants. Salvation, glory, and power belong to God because his judgments are true and just.

Rome has corrupted the nations of the world, seducing them into taking part in her illicit activities. She is also guilty of persecuting the Christian church. In John's day, believers lived under the shadow of the Domitian persecution. They would be encouraged to know that before long God would avenge the oppressive activities of the state. No earthly power—not even the emperor—can kill God's people with impunity. God's judgment will be complete and final—"the smoke [of the city] goes up for ever and ever."

The twenty-four elders and the four living creatures fall down and worship God (as they did when the Lamb received the scroll, 5:6-10). They cry out "Amen" (So let it be!), "Hallelujah" (Praise the Lord!). The overthrow of evil and the vindication of righteousness receive the high praise of heaven. A voice from the throne calls for the servants of God—all who fear him, both small and great—to join in praise. The conflict of the ages is over, and God has prevailed.

**6-10**

John's visions continue. Once again he hears what sounds like the voice of a great multitude. It must have made an unusual impression on him since he describes it further as the roar of rushing waters (a mighty cataract) and as loud peals of thunder. To grasp the overpowering and dramatic effect of this scene, we must imagine ourselves standing at the base of an enormous waterfall or in the midst of a violent thunderstorm.

The heavenly multitude (compare 19:6 with 19:1) praises God because he has taken up his reign and the wedding of the Lamb has come. With the final defeat of sin, the reign of God has been established. While God is eternally sovereign, his control over man and nations is established in the course of history—first by the event of Christ and then at the close of the age by the destruction of sin and Satan.

The concept of a marriage between God and his people has its roots in the Old Testament. Hosea 2:19, for example, records God's promise to Israel: "I will betroth you to me forever." In the New Testament, Paul describes the relationship between Christ and the church with the metaphor of marriage (Eph. 5:32). Now in Revelation, the multitude declares that the wedding of the Lamb has come.

In biblical times marriage involved two events separated by a period of several months. First came the betrothal (legal and binding), and then the wedding itself. The church is now betrothed to Christ. At his return, the wedding will take place.

The bride is adorned in fine linen, bright and clean. She stands in marked contrast to the harlot of chapter 17, who was gaudily dressed in bright colors and expensive accessories (17:4). A parenthetical note explains that "fine linen stands for the righteous acts of the saints."

The adornment of the church consists in her obedient response to the many opportunities for compassion and loving service. This is not a doctrine of salvation by works. It is rather the thoroughly biblical principle that the true people of God must of necessity live transformed lives. They act righteously because they are in fact (in Christ) righteous. A testimony of faith unsupported by a changed life is a fraud.

Verse 9 is the fourth beatitude in Revelation. Blessed are those who are invited to the wedding supper of the Lamb. That believers are both the bride and the wedding guests is typical of apocalyptic language. The literature of Revelation enjoys the freedom of poetic expression, and calls for imagination, not inflexible logic. The wedding supper is not a specific feast that takes place before the millennium. It portrays, rather, the eternal relationship between Christ and those who have accepted his love. The wedding supper lasts forever.

John falls prostrate at the feet of the angel. He would worship this one who has declared blessed all who have been invited to the wedding feast. But John is stopped short by the angel, who says that he is a fellow servant with all those who hold to the witness Jesus bore. God alone is to be worshiped. To this the angel adds that the message attested by Jesus is the essence of prophetic declaration. God is worshiped because he is the one who gives revelation; the angel is simply a mediator and interpreter of visions.

**11-16**

At last John arrives at the central vision of the entire Book of Revelation. The appearance of the Warrior-Messiah marks the end of the old order and the beginning of the new. It is the event for which the contemporary church has patiently waited over the course of some twenty centuries. The heavens stand open to reveal the conquering Messiah and his armies, returning to do battle with his enemies.

A white horse appears. Its rider is named "Faithful and True." The fate of the beast and his followers is compatible with truth and justice. Retribution enacted by the Messiah is neither unfair nor out of line. He judges and makes war with perfect justice.

The first thing to catch John's attention is the rider's eyes, which are like blazing fire. Nothing remains hidden before his piercing gaze. On his head are many royal crowns. His sovereignty is unlimited. He bears a name that no one else knows. Writers have offered a number of suggestions about this name, only to prove what the text itself says: no one but Christ knows or understands the name. It relates to the mystery of his being.

The Messiah is dressed in a robe that has been dipped in blood. While it is tempting to think of this as the blood of Christ shed for the sins of man, in this context the blood is that of his enemies. The imagery recalls a passage in Isaiah when God, in answer to the question, "Why are your garments red?" answers that he has trampled Edom and Bozrah in his anger and "their blood spattered my garments" (Isa. 63:1-6). Apocalyptic imagery is not squeamish.

The rider of the white horse is named "the Word of God." The Hebrews did not think of a word as a lifeless sound but as an active agent that brought about what it declared. In Hebrews 4:12 the word of God is said to be "living and active," "sharper than any double-edged sword." The Warrior-Messiah is God's final *word* to man. When God speaks, his will is actively carried out in time and space.

The armies of heaven, riding white horses and dressed in fine linen, follow their leader. They apparently take no active part in the ensuing warfare. The nations are struck down by a sharp sword that proceeds from the mouth of the Messiah. This sword stands for the word of judgment that Christ speaks (compare 1:16; 2:12, 16). It is unnecessary to expect a literal sword protruding from the mouth of Christ at his Second Coming. We are dealing with apocalyptic images. His word of judgment slays like a mighty sword.

The Messiah will also rule the nations with a rod of iron. As the shepherd carried a stout rod to fend off the attacks of wild beasts, so Christ will destroy all the evil forces that have endangered the church through the ages. He will destroy, not govern, the nations.

Christ will also tread the winepress of the fierce anger of God. His retaliation is pictured in terms of a great flow of blood. God is not a sentimental father who overlooks evil; he is a warrior who passionately hates all sin and injustice. The wrath of God is a thoroughly biblical doctrine and must never be watered down by any well-intentioned attempt to make him more palatable to modern man.

On his robe and on his thigh is the most exalted name imaginable: "KING OF KINGS AND LORD OF LORDS." Handel has captured the grandeur of this title in his magnificent "Hallelujah Chorus." Whatever kings may still be, God is their king. Whatever lords may exist, God is their lord. He rules supreme over all earthly powers. He is lord and master of all creation.

**17-21**

In one way or another, each of the preceding visions in Revelation has brought us closer to the end. Now, just before the final battle, one further vision heightens our suspense. An angel is seen standing in the sun. He delivers a grisly invitation to the birds of prey circling in mid-heaven awaiting the carnage: Come to the great supper of God and gorge yourself on the flesh of man and beast. No one is to be spared. Both free and slave will fall in battle. Even kings and generals will go down. The earth will be covered with the bodies of men and their horses. The prospect of being left on the field of battle at the mercy of predators was abhorrent to the men of old. This grim "supper of God" is a dramatic contrast to the joyful "wedding supper of the Lamb" (v. 9).

Armageddon has arrived. The beast and his armies are matched against the Messiah and his followers. The moment of truth has arrived. But strangely, no conflict is described. Instead, we simply learn that the beast and the false prophet are captured and thrown alive into the fiery lake of burning sulfur. There has never been any real question about the outcome of this final confrontation. Satan was defeated on the cross, and those who prolonged his cause share his defeat.

We will remember that the beast is the personification of secular power in its opposition to righteousness, and the false prophet is pseudoreligion as it persuades men to accept and worship this power. Both are consigned to the lake of fire. Punishment by fire is a common theme in Jewish apocalyptic writing. A lake of fire is mentioned in the Bible only in Revelation. It is undoubtedly the equivalent of hell, Gehenna, a place of fire inhabited by the wicked dead (Mark 9:43-48).

The account closes by noting that the rest were killed by the sword that came out of the Messiah's mouth. The birds descend and gorge themselves on the flesh of fallen men. The gory ordeal is over, and the curtain descends on the stage of history.


## QUESTIONS

1. Why does the great multitude declare that salvation, glory, and power belong to God?
2. How has Rome corrupted the world?
3. What does hallelujah mean?
4. For what two reasons do the great multitude praise God in verses 6-7?
5. What does it mean for the church as the bride of Christ to live in the interim between its engagement to Christ and the wedding ceremony?
6. Of what are the clothes of the church made?
7. With whom is the bride of Christ contrasted?
8. Why does the angel prevent John from worshiping him?

9. What is the "testimony of Jesus"?
10. List the four names of Christ given in verses 11-16. What qualities do they represent?
11. What is intended by the fact that the Messiah's eyes are like blazing fire?
12. Whose blood has stained the Messiah's robe?
13. What is meant by the statement that the Word of God actively brings about what it declares?
14. What is the sword that comes out of the Messiah's mouth?
15. How do you explain the wrath of God in view of the fact that God is love?
16. Who takes part in the great supper of God? With what other supper is it contrasted?
17. Why do you think the final battle is not described?
18. What is the fate of the beast and false prophet?
19. What happens to all who follow the beast in the final conflict?

# REVELATION TWENTY

WE COME NOW to one of the most thoroughly discussed passages in the Book of Revelation. Verses 1-6 teach the doctrine of a millennium (or thousand-year period), during which Satan will be locked up underground in the abyss and Christ with his followers will reign on earth. Interpreters are divided primarily on the basis of whether this reign is taking place now (amillennialism) or whether it will follow the return of Christ (premillennialism). Strong arguments can be marshaled in support of either position.

This commentary adopts the premillennial interpretation. It is more in keeping with the apocalyptic outlook underlying the imagery and thought patterns of the book. And the events of chapter 20 follow in natural sequence the victorious return of the Warrior-Messiah in chapter 19. The history of interpretation shows that amillennialism arose not so much as a straightforward attempt to explain the text but as an allegorical reaction to the extreme literalism of certain groups in the third- and fourth-century church.

**1-3**

An angel descends from heaven with the key to the abyss (an underground cavern that housed evil spirits awaiting judgment, see Jude 6). In his hand is a great chain. The angel seizes the devil, binds him, throws him into the abyss, and then locks and seals the entrance. He is held securely for the next thousand years. The purpose of this restriction is that he might not deceive the nations any longer. Following this period of retention, he is to be set free for a short time.

Satan is described by four different titles. Not only is he Satan (the adversary), but he is also the devil (the accuser), the dragon (who, defeated in heavenly combat, vents his wrath against the church, 12:7-17), and that ancient serpent (who deceived Eve in the garden of Eden, Genesis 3). His names reveal his true nature.

**4-6**

John sees thrones, which are occupied by those who have received the authority to judge. The text does not indicate who they are, or make clear exactly what they are to judge. They may be a heavenly court that is some-how connected with the great, white-throne judgment in verses 11-15.

John also sees the souls of those who had been exe-cuted for their faithful witness to Jesus and the word of God. They are further described as not having wor-shiped the beast or his image. Neither did they receive his mark on their foreheads or hands. These martyrs are the souls under the altar (fifth seal, 6:9-11), who cried out to God to avenge their blood. They represent all who have given their lives in faithful obedience to God. It is with this group that the millennium deals.

The martyrs are said to come to life and reign with Christ for a thousand years. It is crucial to determine what "come to life" means in this context.

Those who interpret the millennium in a nonliteral sense (amillennialists) hold that it means to be resurrected from a state of spiritual death. Verses such as Colossians 3:1 ("Since, then, you have been raised with Christ") are used in support. From this it would follow that to reign with Christ means to share with him in the present age his sovereign control over the earth.

It is more natural to take the verb to mean a return to life in a physical sense. In Revelation 2:8 Christ is described as the one who "died and came to life again" (same verb). Jairus's daughter had died, but he knew that if Jesus touched her she would live (Matt. 9:18).

The most powerful argument that verse 4 speaks of a physical resurrection is that in the very next verse the same verb is used to speak of the bodily resurrection that follows the millennium. There is no suggestion in the text itself that this verb should be interpreted in two widely different ways in these adjacent passages.

Readers often ask if the thousand years should be taken as a literal period of time. It has been said that unless the plain sense makes nonsense, seek no further sense. This would encourage us to take the thousand years as one thousand actual years of 365 days each.

On the other hand, most of the numbers we have encountered thus far in Revelation have been symbolic. Seven designates completeness. The number 144,000 is a multiple of 12, the number of the tribes of Israel and the disciples of Christ. In either case, one thousand years would be an extended period of time, during which Christ and the martyred saints would carry out their reign.

But what is the purpose of the millennium? The usual premillennial answer is that it displays within history the victory of righteousness over evil. However, if it is true that the millennium relates to Christian martyrs rather than the church at large, another explanation is to be preferred. In chapter 6 the martyrs are told to wait under the altar until their number is complete; then their blood will be avenged upon the hostile world (6:9-11). According to this interpretation, the millennium is a special reward to those who have given their lives in faithful opposition to the demands of the Antichrist. During their lifetime they were under the heel of tyranny; when Christ returns in victory, the tables will be turned, and the faithful will rule over their oppressors.

Is it necessary for the millennium to take place in history or are we to understand it in terms of what it symbolizes? Since a promise must always be couched in the language of its own time, it may be that the millennium (like "streets of gold") will be realized in different terms. In either case it will be the ultimate vindication of all who have gone down under the sword of the state.

By placing the first sentence of verse 5 in parenthesis, the NIV has correctly identified the first resurrection as that of the martyrs. If it is true that the millennium is the vindication of actual martyrs (rather than the entire church), then the "rest of the dead" who are raised after the thousand years would include both believer and unbeliever. In either case, a blessing is pronounced on those who have a part in the first resurrection. The second death (defined as "the lake of fire") has no power over them. Their lot is to serve as priests of God and to rule with Christ for a thousand years.

**7-10**

At the close of the millennial period, Satan is released from his prison. True to his nature, he goes out to deceive the nations into following him into battle against the people of God. The most reasonable explanation of this unexpected turn of events is that God wishes to demonstrate one more time that Satan's evil purpose will never change, and that human nature is not altered with the passing of time.

Gog and Magog are singled out as examples of nations who join Satan's last revolt. In Ezekiel 38 and 39, however, Gog is a prince who leads an invasion against Israel, and according to Genesis 10:2, Magog is one of the sons of Japeth. This shift from personal names to nations should cause no problem. In Revelation Gog and Magog are symbolic of all nations that join in the final assault upon God and his people.

So successful is Satan in his deceit and cunning that those who follow him are in number like the sand on the seashore. They march across the breadth of the earth and surround the camp of God's people. Once again, no battle is described. Fire comes down from heaven and devours the entire army. The devil is not consumed by the fire but is thrown into the lake of burning sulfur to join the beast and the false prophet (19:20). The unholy trinity is tormented day and night for ever and ever. The text provides no support for a doctrine of limited punishment followed by annihilation. Scripture teaches the eternal suffering of the damned.

**11-14**

The time for final judgment has come. John sees a great, white throne. The one seated upon the throne is undoubtedly God the Father, although on the basis of such verses as John 5:22 some have held the judge to be

Christ. Earth and sky flee from his presence. Depending upon the degree of literalness adopted by the interpreter, this is either a poetic way of expressing creation's reaction to the majesty of God or a description of the physical dissolution of the universe (perhaps in preparation for the new heaven and earth shortly to appear, 21:1).

All the dead stand before the throne awaiting judgment. The books are opened. The dead are judged according to what they have done as recorded in the books. Final judgment is not arbitrary. It is based squarely upon the record of a man's life. Note that John is not teaching a doctrine of salvation by works. Salvation is based upon one's faith in the gracious redemptive activity of Christ. It is the reality of that faith as expressed in a life of good works that is judged (see Rom. 2:6; 1 Pet. 1:17). We are saved by grace but judged by our works.

In addition to the books that record the deeds of men, "another book was opened, which is the book of life" (v. 12b). While the relationship between these books is not absolutely clear, there is no doubt that the book of life is also involved in the judgment process. Verse 15 says that those whose names are not found in the book of life will be cast into the lake of fire.

No one escapes judgment. The sea gives up its dead as do death and Hades (the abode of the wicked dead). Once again we read that "each person was judged according to what he had done" (v. 13; see also v. 12). Then all the wicked are thrown into the lake of fire along with death and Hades. Sin is forever put away, and everything associated with it is assigned to eternal punishment—Satan, who first rebelled against God; the beast and false prophet, who carried out his evil designs in history; the men of the world who chose to worship

Satan; death, his last weapon; and Hades, Satan's appropriate domain. The victory of God is complete.


## QUESTIONS

1. Describe the imprisonment of Satan. Does this sound like a partial restriction of his activity (his condition during the present church age), or complete removal from the affairs of men? Why?
2. What are the four titles given Satan in verse 2? What does each mean?
3. Where in Revelation did we first meet the Christian martyrs? Why were they put to death?
4. What does it mean that the martyrs "came to life"? What are the arguments that favor this point of view?
5. How long is the "thousand years" of Revelation 20?
6. List two possible purposes for the millennium. Which do you favor? Why?
7. If the martyrs are raised in the first resurrection, who is raised in the second resurrection?
8. What is the "second death"?
9. Which do you think more probable, an actual thousand-year reign of the martyrs or a nontemporal and figurative fulfillment of the millennium? Why?
10. Why does God release Satan after a thousand years?
11. What do Gog and Magog stand for in the Revelation passage?
12. What expression in Revelation 20 argues eternal torment of the damned rather than annihilation?
13. On what basis does God judge men?
14. What purpose is served by the book of life?
15. Where does all evil finally end up?

# REVELATION
# TWENTY-ONE

THE FINAL CHAPTERS of Revelation are radically different from the scenes of judgment we have just passed through. With the removal of sin, the atmosphere is totally transformed. The remaining chapters radiate the joy of the coming age. They present the new heaven and the new earth, with only an occasional backward glance at those who choose to dwell outside the city of God (21:8; 22:11, 15). God's promise to "create new heavens and a new earth" (Isa. 65:17) is fulfilled in the descent of the heavenly Jerusalem to take its place on a renewed earth.

**1-4**

The renovation of the old order is a common theme in

apocalyptic literature. Peter looked forward to the day when the heavens would be destroyed by fire, and the elements would melt in the heat. They are to be replaced by a new heaven and a new earth in which righteousness dwells (2 Pet. 3:10-13). John now sees the final outcome of this transformation. The sea, which was connected with all matter of evil (the beast came out of the sea; 13:1, 6-7), has no place in the new order.

John watches the new Jerusalem ("the Holy City") as it descends from heaven. It is adorned as a bride for her husband. The new Jerusalem symbolizes the people of God in their perfected and eternal state. It emphasizes the fact that the church universal is a community of redeemed individuals living together in love.

A loud voice from the throne declares that God's dwelling is with man. The Greek word *skene* (tabernacle) is closely related to the Hebrew *shekinah* (the presence and glory of God). God himself in all his glory has come to take up his eternal residence with faithful believers. As the text says, "And he will live [tabernacle, *skenosei*] with them . . . and be their God." This is the essence of heaven—not streets of gold or mansions of glory. Unbroken fellowship is the central feature of the eternal state.

God will wipe away every tear. These are not tears of remorse but the lingering effects of having lived in a sinful world. The old order with its death and mourning, crying and pain, has passed away. The new and perfect order of eternal joy has taken its place.

**5-8**

God declares from his throne that he is making everything new. The old order marred by sin dissolves into the past. He orders John to write down his words for they are trustworthy and true. Future blessedness has become present reality. "It is done," he exclaims. Sin is forever put away, and righteousness dwells throughout the new heaven and earth.

God is Alpha and Omega (the first and last letters of the Greek alphabet). He is the source of all things and their ultimate goal. He is "the Beginning and the End." To all who are thirsty, God gives "to drink without cost from the spring of the water of life." He promises spiritual refreshment and eternal felicity to all who come with thirst to him. He will accept the overcomer as his son and will be his God. All these metaphors add dimension and meaning to our understanding of what awaits the faithful in the world to come.

In contrast to the eternal family of God are those who, having chosen to join forces with the enemy, end up in the lake of fire. Many—perhaps all—of those listed in verse 8 may be interpreted as professing Christians who gave up the faith. The cowardly drew back from following Christ when the going got rough. The unbelieving denied their faith under pressure. The vile have been polluted with the defilements of emperor worship. The sexually immoral fell into the major vice of paganism. These apostates (and the others mentioned in verse 8) have their place in the fiery lake of burning sulfur. The second death forever seals their doom. The purpose of this catalog of vices is to stress by contrast the righteous character of God's chosen people.

**9-14**

One of the angels who poured out the seven bowls of God's wrath now invites John to come and see the bride, the wife of the Lamb. The invitation parallels 17:1, in which the angel invited John to witness the punishment of the great whore. This calls attention to the contrast between the bride and the harlot. The new Jerusalem descends from heaven and represents all that is sacred and beautiful. Rome symbolized the evil and wickedness of human civilization here on earth.

To watch the descent of the holy city, John is carried away in the Spirit to a great high mountain. Mountains have always played an important role in God's dealings with man. Moses received the commandments on. Mount Sinai (Exodus 20). Ezekiel's vision of a restored Israel came when he was on "a very high mountain" (Ezek. 40: 2). Christ left his followers from the Mount of Olives and to that mountaintop he will return (Acts 1: 9-12).

The bride that John is to see turns out to be a city. The metaphors of the apocalyptic are mixed and show little inclination to conform to any rigid system of interpretation. The faithful are portrayed not only as the bride of the Lamb but also as the eternal city in which God is to dwell.

The holy city is aglow with the glory of God. It sparkles with the brilliance of precious jewels. A great, high wall symbolizes complete security. The city has twelve gates, inscribed with the names of the twelve tribes of Israel, and twelve foundations, upon which are written the names of the twelve apostles of the Lamb. It is obvious that by this imagery the author wishes to emphasize the continuity between Israel of old and the New Testament church. God's people from all ages share together in the glorious age to come. Twelve gates suggest abundant entrance and twelve foundations, with the names of the twelve apostles, remind us that the church is built upon the witness of the apostles and prophets (see Matt. 16: 18; Eph. 2: 20).

**15-17**

The angel in charge of showing John the new Jerusalem has a rod of gold with which he measures the city, its gates and its walls. The city is laid out like a square, as long as it is wide. But in the same verse it is also said to be "as wide and high as it is long." This means that the city of John's vision is a cube. This shape would immediately remind the Jewish reader of the inner sanctuary of the temple, a perfect cube measuring some thirty feet in each direction. The presence of God dwelt in this most holy place. A city shaped like a cube would symbolize God's eternal dwelling with man.

The enormous size of the city has caused some surprise. Since a *stadion* is about 607 feet, 1,200 *stadia* would be approximately 1,400 miles. While it is possible to conceive of a city covering the entire territory of the United States west of the Mississippi, it is difficult to think of the same city reaching 1,400 miles up into the ionosphere. The numbers are obviously symbolic. They portray the new Jerusalem as an enormous city; we are not to take them as specific measurements.

The same can be said of the walls of the city, which are 144 cubits (about 216 feet) high. The number 144 is the square of 12 (the number of tribes and apostles) and apparently was chosen for that reason. (Two-hundred-foot walls around a city more than 7 million feet high would be a bit out of proportion!)

**18-21**

The wall of the city is made of jasper, while the city itself is of pure gold. The foundations of the wall are inlaid with every kind of precious stone. Although it is difficult to identify and catalog the gems of antiquity with any precision, the stones listed would probably reflect such colors as green, blue, red, white, yellow, and purple. The gates of the wall are made of single pearls, and the street is pure gold. The overall impression is one of beauty and brilliance. The city is magnificent. It is the dwelling place of God.

**22-27**

A great truth is enshrined in the fact that no temple

exists in the eternal city because "the Lord God Almighty and the Lamb are its temple." Symbol has given way to reality. The temporary forms that belong to time have no continuing purpose in eternity. God and the Lamb are the temple. None other is needed. Nor does the city need sun or moon. It is illuminated by the glory of God. The Lamb is its source of light.

Verses 24-26 present a small problem. Who are the nations walking by its light and the kings of the earth bringing their splendor into it? Who are the impure who will never enter its gates? (The problem arises in 22:2, 15 as well.)

The answer is that John is speaking of the future in terms of his own historical existence. The references are not intended to teach that in the age to come certain people from the outside will have limited access to heaven. Rather, the eternal city is described for the moment as if it belonged to this earthly sphere of existence.

To say that kings and nations bring their tribute to the heavenly Jerusalem is to underscore the prominence and prosperity of the city. Its gates will never be shut because evil will no longer exist. There will be perfect security. That which is impure, shameful, and deceitful will be forever removed from the city. Only those whose names are written in the Lamb's book of life will enter.

## QUESTIONS

1. What does it mean for a city to be adorned as a bride awaiting her husband?
2. What or who is symbolized by the new Jerusalem?
3. From verse 3 how would you describe the essence of heaven?
4. How do you account for tears in heaven? Do you

find tears and joy incompatible?

5. What is claimed by the title Alpha and Omega?
6. What reward is given the overcomer (v. 7)? Can you imagine anything of greater value? Can this relationship be enjoyed at least in part before the end of time?
7. What is the second death?
8. How is it that the bride of the Lamb may be described as a city?
9. Why do you suppose that the eternal state is described in terms of a city made of gold and precious stones? If John were writing today, would he use the same images?
10. What is suggested by the fact that the twelve tribes and the twelve apostles are mentioned in close connection?
11. What is the basic significance of the fact that the new Jerusalem is shaped like a cube?
12. Why are the numbers 12,000 *stadia* and 144 cubits to be taken symbolically at this point?
13. Why is a temple unnecessary in the new Jerusalem?
14. Explain why the text speaks of nations existing outside the city in the eternal age.
15. On what basis does a person gain entrance to the eternal city?

# REVELATION
# TWENTY-TWO

THE OPENING OF A NEW chapter at this point tends to obscure the fact that the description of the new Jerusalem that began at 21:9 continues on through the fifth verse of chapter 22.

**1-5**

The guiding angel (see 21:9, 15) shows John a river, clear as crystal, flowing from the heavenly throne down the center of a wide boulevard. The river of the water of life flows from the throne of God and the Lamb. Note that the throne belongs to both of them. On either side of the river stands a tree of life, bearing twelve different kinds of fruit and yielding a fresh crop each month. God's provisions for man in the heavenly city are varied and abundant.

Not only does the tree of life provide fruit for enjoyment, but its leaves are for the healing of the nations. This detail does not imply that in the age to come all the nations of the world will be healed from the sickness of sin. As we noted before (21:24-27), this kind of reference simply carries over into the eternal state imagery that belongs to the present age. The point John wishes to make is that there will be no disease in heaven. Nor will there be any curse.

God and the Lamb will rule the eternal city. The faithful will serve God; their greatest joy will be the exalted privilege of seeing his face. In ancient times, criminals were banished from the realm so they could never again see the face of the king (see Esther 7:8). To see God is a blessing reserved for the pure in heart (Matt. 5:8), and will be fully experienced only when we are transformed into his likeness (1 John 3:2).

Night will be no more. There will be no need of either lamp or sun because the radiance of God will illuminate every portion of the heavenly city. It is in this place of beauty and splendor that the church of Jesus Christ is to reign for ever and ever.

**6-7**

Verses 6 through 21 constitute an epilogue to the entire series of visions that make up the Book of Revelation. You will notice a number of similarities between the epilogue and the prologue (for instance, the book is a genuine prophecy, 1:3 with 22:6; it is to be read in the churches, 1:11 with 22:18; and it is for the encouragement of the faithful, 1:3 with 22:12).

The angel declares that the visions of things to come are trustworthy and true. They merit our confidence because they correspond to reality. The source of revelation is God, who quickens the spirits of the prophets. The angel was sent by God to show his servants the things that "must soon take place." It has troubled some interpreters that from John's position in history these things apparently did not take place "soon." Some two thousand years have gone by and the end is not yet.

The most satisfactory answer to this problem is that since the beginning of the church era, we have been in the last days (Heb. 1:2). Down through history, the end has always been imminent in the sense that at any point in time this age could rapidly draw to a close. This fact has lent an air of urgency to the church's mission of evangelism. From God's perspective, time is not a sequence of passing moments but an accommodation to the limitations of creation. He himself inhabits eternity. He was, he is, he shall be.

It is also helpful to note that predictive prophecy regularly involves a telescoping of time. The great redemptive events of God in time are brought together in the perspective of the prophet. Thus the consummation towards which history inevitably moves is always imminent in prophetic declaration.

Jesus speaks: "Behold, I am coming soon!" (vv. 7, 12). This truth in times of stress has brought great encouragement to faithful believers. In times of rejoicing, it has heightened the church's anticipation of the glorious age to come.

The two last beatitudes in Revelation (there are seven altogether) are found in chapter 22. The first (v. 7) pronounces a blessing upon those who obey the prophetic message contained in the book. Prophecy is not given so that believers will be able to develop an elaborate chronology of the last days, but so they will be obedient to its ethical implications. The primary goal is to change conduct, not to inform the intellect.

**8-9**

John, the author of Revelation, attests that he has

163

heard and seen the things about which he has written. They are not literary creations developed to communicate religious insights. John is a recorder of actual visions; he is not a creative visionary. He falls at the feet of the angel who has been his guide with the intention of worshiping him (curious, in view of 19:10). But the angel prevents him, indicating that he, too, is a servant of God, along with John and all those who obey the words of the prophecy. God alone is worthy of worship.

**10-11**

At an earlier time, the prophet Daniel was told to "close up and seal the words of the scroll until the time of the end" (Dan. 12:4). But now that time has come, so John is told, "Do not seal up the words of the prophecy of this book." From the perspective of the seer, the end is so near that there is no longer time for men to change their habits or alter their character. The destiny of each has been determined by how he has lived his life. The wrong will continue to do wrong.

Equally true is the fact that those who do right will continue to do right, and those who are holy will continue in holiness. The future has been determined by the way each has lived. There exists no possibility of a last-minute transformation.

**12-13**

Again we hear Christ declare that he is coming soon. He brings with him his reward and distributes it on the basis of what each person has done. In 20:12, judgment depended on the record of what men had done. Now we learn that rewards are given on the same basis. Perfect justice will be enacted because the One who distributes the rewards has complete knowledge: he is "the Alpha and the Omega . . . the Beginning and the End."

**14-15**

The final beatitude of the book is pronounced on

those who are washing (the present time suggests a continual washing) their robes. They steadfastly refuse the temptation to soil their garments by compromising with sin and Satan. As a result, they have a right to the tree of life. Eternal life is the reward for faithfulness under trial. Or, put another way, they may pass through the gates and on into the city of God.

Not so the wicked. Outside the city are all manner of evil persons—dogs (the unclean), sorcerers, the sexually immoral, murderers, idolaters, and deceivers. No sinner of any sort will have a place within the eternal city. As we learned elsewhere (20:15), their end will be the lake of fire.

**16**

Jesus authenticates the angel who has guided John through the various visions of Revelation. The message has been for the churches. It is intended for encouragement and direction in times of stress. It assures the church universal that God is sovereign and will at the end of time destroy every vestige of wickedness and usher in the eternal age of righteousness.

By naming himself "the Root and the Offspring of David," Jesus lays claim to the messianic promise given through the prophet Isaiah (Isa. 11:1, 10). He is also "the bright Morning Star" (see Num. 24:17) that heralds the end of the long night of tribulation and the dawn of a new day of eternal joy.

**17**

This verse is a multiple invitation. The Spirit (the Holy Spirit) and the bride (the church) say "Come!" Those who hear echo the invitation. Whoever is thirsty may come. Whoever wishes may take as a free gift the water of life. Readers of the Old Testament will recognize a similar invitation extended by Isaiah, "Come, all you who are thirsty. . . . Come, buy wine and milk

WHAT ARE WE WAITING FOR?

without money and without cost" (Isa. 55:1). The invitation in Revelation is general and extends to all who will hear the words of the prophecy.

**18-19**

John brings his work to a close with a severe warning against tampering with its contents. He warns that if anyone adds to the words of the prophecy, God will add to him the plagues described in the book. If anyone takes words away from the prophecy, God will take away from him his share in the tree of life and in the holy city as described in the book.

The revelation of God's victory over evil, the return of Christ, the punishment of the wicked, and the eternal blessedness of the righteous—all will take place exactly as described. There is no possibility of the slightest change. For man to alter the prophecy by addition would be to involve God in saying something he never intended. To take away from the prophecy would be to deny God the right to say something he wants to say. Hence the seriousness of the warning. (It is a warning that should cause every commentator on Revelation to do his prayerful best in telling others what the book is all about!)

**20**

Revelation began with the promise that the consummation of history would "soon take place" (1:1). It closes with Christ's promise, "Yes, I am coming soon." John adds, "Amen. Come, Lord Jesus." This prayer expresses the central hope of all faithful believers. It is the equivalent of the Aramaic *maranatha* (Our Lord, come!) of 1 Corinthians 16:22, RSV.

**21**

Although Revelation is an apocalypse, it began as an epistle (1:4) and ends accordingly with a benediction. The benediction was first pronounced upon all those believers in the seven churches of Asia who listened while the book was read aloud. It now extends to all who love his appearing. From John's day until ours it has bestowed the grace of the Lord Jesus upon those who have steadfastly refused to be taken in by the propaganda of Satan or be intimidated by his threats. The people of God are those who have emerged victorious from the battle of faith. They are the overcomers who, in the face of persecution, have reaffirmed their commitment to the Lamb of God and his redemptive work in history.

## QUESTIONS

1. What is symbolized by a tree that yields twelve kinds of fruit every month?
2. Why will seeing the face of God be the essence of eternal life? What keeps us from wanting this experience while in our present state?
3. Explain in your own words why the promise of a quick return of Christ in view of the intervening 2,000 years is not a basic contradiction.
4. Why do you suppose John tried to worship the angel in 22:8 after he had been stopped from doing the very same thing earlier (19:10)?
5. Why was John not to seal up the prophecy?
6. On what basis will Christ distribute rewards when he returns?
7. In the context of verse 14, what does it mean to wash one's robes?
8. What is involved in Christ's claim that he is "the Root and the Offspring of David"?
9. In what sense is Christ the "Morning Star"?
10. What kind of alterations to Revelation would fall

under the curse of verses 18 and 19?

11. How do you account for the seriousness of the warning?

12. Explain the fact that an apocalypse closes with a benediction.